User Satisfaction with Personalised Internet Applications

Forschungsergebnisse der Wirtschaftsuniversität Wien

Band 27

PETER LANG
Frankfurt am Main · Berlin · Bern · Bruxelles · New York · Oxford · Wien

Ulrike Bauernfeind

User Satisfaction with Personalised Internet Applications

PETER LANG
Internationaler Verlag der Wissenschaften

Bibliographic Information published by the Deutsche Nationalbibliothek
The Deutsche Nationalbibliothek lists this publication in the Deutsche Nationalbibliografie; detailed bibliographic data is available in the internet at <http://www.d-nb.de>.

Cover design:
Atelier Platen according to a design of the advertising agency Publique.

University logo of the Vienna University of Economics and Business Administration.
Printed with kindly permission of the University.

Sponsored by the Vienna University of Economics and Business Administration.

ISSN 1613-3056
ISBN 978-3-631-57770-7

www.peterlang.de

TABLE OF CONTENTS

1 **INTRODUCTION** **13**

1.1 Problem statement 13

1.2 Objectives of the study 15

1.3 Structure of the book 15

2 **STATE OF THE FIELD – THEORETICAL BACKGROUND** **19**

2.1 Classification of Personalised Internet Applications 19

2.2 Relevant Research Traditions and Theories 24

2.3 Customer Satisfaction in General 26

2.4 Human-Computer Interaction (HCI) 28

2.4.1 The Technology Acceptance Model (TAM) 29
2.4.2 The IS Success Model 36
2.4.3 Flow 38
2.4.4 Hedonic aspects 41
2.4.5 Other Approaches 48

2.5 User Interface Design Aspects 50

2.6 System Evaluation 52

2.6.1 Software Evaluation Methods 52
2.6.2 Web Site Evaluation Methods 57

3 **INFLUENCES ON PERSONALISED INTERNET APPLICATIONS' SATISFACTION – RESEARCH MODEL AND HYPOTHESES** **61**

3.1 Research Model 61

3.2 Influencing Factors – Constructs and Hypotheses 63

3.2.1 Perceived Usefulness 64
3.2.2 Perceived Ease of Use 65
3.2.3 Trust 66
3.2.4 Exploratory Browsing Behaviour 67

3.2.5 Enjoyment ... 68
3.2.6 Attitude towards e-service ... 69
3.2.7 Experience ... 70
3.2.8 Satisfaction ... 71
3.2.9 Commitment ... 72

4 STUDY METHODOLOGY ... 73

4.1 Research Methods ... 73

4.1.1 Qualitative versus quantitative research methods ... 73
4.1.2 Approaches Used in this Study ... 74

4.2 Development of the Survey Instrument ... 74

4.3 Internet Applications Used for Evaluation ... 78

4.3.1 Tiscover ... 80
4.3.2 Learn@WU ... 80
4.3.3 Immobilien.net ... 81

4.4 Study Participants ... 81

4.5 Experimental setting and data collection method ... 82

5 EMPIRICAL RESULTS ... 85

5.1 Descriptive Statistics ... 85

5.1.1 Demographic Description of the Sample ... 86
5.1.2 Personal Characteristics of the Sample ... 87
5.1.3 Comparison of the three Personalised Internet Applications ... 92

5.2 Testing the Structural Model of Satisfaction with Personalised Internet Applications ... 108

5.2.1 Formative versus Reflective Indicators ... 109
5.2.2 Measurement and Structural Model ... 111
5.2.3 Model Evaluation in SEM ... 113
5.2.4 Results of Testing the Structural Hypotheses ... 117
5.2.5 Structural Analyses for the three Personalised Internet Applications ... 131

5.3 Expert Interviews ... 139

5.3.1 Method of Expert Interviews ... 140
5.3.2 Results of Expert Interviews ... 141

6 DISCUSSION AND OUTLOOK **151**

6.1 Conclusion 151

6.2 Implications for Practitioners 152

6.3 Limitations and Implications for Future Research 153

References **155**

Appendix **175**

LIST OF TABLES

Table 1. Selected TAM-Related Contributions 32

Table 2. Selected IS Success Model-Related Contributions 36

Table 3. Selected Flow-related Approaches 40

Table 4. Hedonic – Utilitarian Scale 43

Table 5. Goal-directed and Experiential Online Behaviour 44

Table 6. Overview of Other HCI Approaches 49

Table 7. Classification of Software Evaluation Methods 53

Table 8. An overview of PUTQ areas 55

Table 9. Web Site Evaluation Methods by Categories 59

Table 10. Constructs and their Measurement Items 75

Table 11. Classification of the Personalised Internet Applications Tested ... 80

Table 12. Test Tasks for the Respective Internet Applications 82

Table 13. Sample Size 86

Table 14. Demographic Characteristics of Respondents 87

Table 15. Self-assessment of WWW Experience 89

Table 16. Items for the Construct "Ease of Use" 92

Table 17. Overall Ease of Use 93

Table 18. Items for the Construct "Usefulness" 94

Table 19. Usefulness of the Web Sites 95

Table 20. Items for the Construct "Enjoyment" 97

Table 21. Does the Web Site Create New Ideas? 98

Table 22. Items for the Construct "Exploratory Browsing Behaviour" 98

Table 23. Novelty of Information or Products 100

Table 24. Overall Ratings for Exploratory Browsing Behaviour Items 101

Table 25. Items for the Construct "Trust" 102
Table 26. Perceived Security Standards 103
Table 27. Items for the Construct "Satisfaction" 104
Table 28. Positive Experience with the Web Site 106
Table 29. Items for the Construct "Commitment" 106
Table 30. Intention to Revisit the Web Site 107
Table 31. Recommended Model Fits in SEM 115
Table 32. Final Scales 117
Table 33. Reliability and Validity 123
Table 34. Shared Variance to Assess Discriminant Validity 125
Table 35. Fit Indices for the Measurement Model 126
Table 36. Fit Indices for the Structural Model 128
Table 37. Path Estimates for Multiple Group Analysis 132
Table 38. Multiple Group Analysis: Critical Ratios and p-level 133
Table 39. Multiple Group Analysis – Differences in Chi-Square 134
Table 40. Ease of Use Issues Named by Experts 143
Table 41. Usefulness Issues Named by Experts 144
Table 42. Trust Issues Named by Experts 146
Table 43. Opinions on Exploratory Browsing Behaviour 148
Table 44. Further Crucial Issues 149

LIST OF FIGURES

Figure 1. Personalisation Techniques 21
Figure 2. The Consumer Decision Making Process 23
Figure 3. The Theory of Reasoned Action 29
Figure 4. Theory of Planned Behaviour 30
Figure 5. The original Technology Acceptance Model 31
Figure 6. TAM and Possible Influencing Factors 35
Figure 7. Flow and its Direct Influences in CME 38
Figure 8. Pleasure and Arousal Components 46
Figure 9. Concepts of Hedonic Motivated User Behaviour 48
Figure 10. Examples of Data Collection Methods for Usability Testing 56
Figure 11. Three Areas of Webmining 58
Figure 12. Components of the Conceptual Model 62
Figure 13. The Research Model 63
Figure 14. Average Use of the WWW 88
Figure 15. Self-assessment of Web Site Familiarity 89
Figure 16. The Usefulness of the WWW for the Task 90
Figure 17. Usefulness of Obtaining Information via the WWW 91
Figure 18. Learnability of the Web Sites 93
Figure 19. Facilitation of the Searching Process through Online Resources 96
Figure 20. Inspiration of the Web Sites 99
Figure 21. Trust towards the Information 102
Figure 22. Overall, how is your Impression of this Web Site? 105
Figure 23. Do you Intend to Recommend the Web Site? 108
Figure 24. Formative Indicators 110

Figure 25. Reflective Indicators 111
Figure 26. Structural Equation Model (adapted from Backhaus 2003) 112
Figure 27. Overview of Categories of Fit Measures 113
Figure 28. Measurement Model for the Independent Variables 121
Figure 29. Measurement Model for the Dependent Variables 122
Figure 30. Overall Structural Model Explaining Satisfaction 127
Figure 31. Alternative Structural Model with Enjoyment 129
Figure 32. Alternative Structural Model 130
Figure 33. Partial Structural Model for Tiscover 136
Figure 34. Partial Structural Model for Immobilien.net 137
Figure 35. Partial Structural Model for Learn@WU 138

1 INTRODUCTION

The WWW changed from a purely information retrieval function towards a place where customers are increasingly buying products and services. The figures estimated for the US growth in online purchases during the time period 2004 to 2008 amount to 18.5%. For some European countries like the UK, Germany, France, Italy and Spain the estimation of growth is even much higher with 41% for the same time period 2004-2008 (eMarketer, 2005).

On the one hand, people use the Internet more and more for purchasing goods. On the other hand, there is an overwhelming amount of information about products and services constituting the need for improved functions to help internet users being efficient. Personalised systems and recommender systems offer the useful functionality to provide search results and proposals tailored to the individual preferences and constraints of the user. Personalisation (or customisation) is defined as a technique proposing individualised content for each customer (Greer & Murtaza, 2003). Personalised and recommender systems filter out relevant items for a customer according to his or her previously stated preferences and needs (Thompson, Göker, & Langley, 2004).

Compared to stand-alone web sites those kind of online systems offer the advantage for the customer to reduce search costs (Lynch & Ariely, 2000). Furthermore, personalised systems help to decrease information overload and to increase user loyalty (Perugini, Gonçalves, & Fox, 2004).

1.1 Problem statement

Research investigating Human-Computer Interaction (HCI) concepts applied to personalised systems and recommenders is very limited disregarding the fact that the significance of those systems increases more and more. Additionally, new factors, like trust emerge, whose significance was not that high in the past. Purchase activities require websites which provide the user with a feeling of security if required to give away personal and sensitive data like credit card information. The influence of trust was considered in various studies, e.g. Koufaris and Hampton-Sosa (2004), Gefen and Straub (2004). Their findings suggest that trust has a significant impact on online purchase intentions.

Another important development is that people are more and more experienced when using the Internet. Rising internet experience leads to higher expectations and satiation effects. Not only utilitarian but also hedonic benefits are sought. It is not enough anymore to have a website offering necessary information which can be easily found. Satiation effects require additional appeals, e.g. fun during the purchasing process. Purchasing and browsing activities on the Internet should fulfil a kind of entertainment function as well. There are already a number of studies investigating the effect of fun, enjoyment, playfulness or pleasurefulness. Yi and Hwang (2003) highlighted the importance of enjoyment as antecedent of usefulness, ease of use and self-efficacy. Van der Heijden (2003) added the construct perceived enjoyment to ease of use and usefulness (which are the two factors of the Technology Acceptance Model (TAM)). Chung and Tan (2004) investigated the antecedents of perceived playfulness which are among others, speed, content, variety, focused attention. Teo, Lim et al. (1999) found out that most importantly, the Internet is regarded useful for task fulfilment and second, there is surprisingly already enjoyment together with ease of use.

Technical and skill barriers did have a significant influence on the use of and on the satisfaction with the Internet. However, these influencing factors are diminishing more and more; technical and skill barriers are less and less inhibitors to use the Internet for purchase activities. Bandwidth is constantly being improved. More and more people have access to the Internet and therefore become more skilled. Together, these factors contribute to a rapid change in the Internet "environment". Thus, the goal of this study is to combine those changing and emerging factors in a common model for explaining satisfaction with personalised internet applications.

This study distinguishes from already existing ones by the following aspects: First, the focus will not be on the measurement of general WWW satisfaction and its influencing factors. Instead, three particular personalised internet applications are investigated. The satisfaction is measured directly after the users have experienced the system and have finished a predetermined task simulating real problem solving and purchasing activities. When measuring such emotional constructs like exploratory browsing or enjoyment it is crucial to conduct an evaluation immediately after the experience with a particular web site has taken place because memories are fading. An explanatory model for the satisfaction with personalised internet applications was proposed, elaborated and tested in the course of this study. Furthermore, the influencing factors trust and exploratory browsing behaviour were added in the satisfaction model additionally to ease of use and usefulness.

1.2 Objectives of the study

The predominant goal pursued with this study is to develop a comprehensive model which is appropriate to evaluate satisfaction with personalised internet applications. What are the main factors driving satisfaction which in turn influences commitment (the intention to revisit the web site or to recommend it to others)?

Furthermore, the study has several sub goals. First, literature is reviewed to identify similar studies and relevant approaches from other web site studies, information systems (IS) and Human-Computer Interaction (HCI) studies. The main objective of this step is to identify possible influencing factors. Second, a research model is proposed based on those influencing factors. For each of the model dimensions measurement items are developed either by literature review or in an exploratory manner (by proposing new items and pre-testing them). Third, the research model is tested among users (test persons) involving three different personalised internet applications stemming from different areas. The reason for that is the objective to develop a model covering influencing factors for a wider range of personalised internet applications. The survey will be Internet based because test persons are asked to experience the web site before evaluating it. A major concern is that a certain kind of involvement is created by proposing them to accomplish a pre-determined task and to reduce extraneous variance. The goal was to collect a rather large sample size of more than 1000 test persons to be able to analyse the survey data with structural equation modelling, to employ multiple group analysis and to discover differences among the personalised internet applications.

1.3 Structure of the book

This study aims to investigate the influencing factors on satisfaction with personalised internet applications. The book consists of six chapters starting with the introduction. The theoretical background relevant to this study is described next. The research model, the study methodology and the results are presented in the following chapters. Finally, the conclusion drawn from this study as well as implications for practitioners and future research are outlined.

The theoretical background chapter starts with a classification of personalised internet applications. What is the difference to ordinary web sites or more sophisticated systems like recommenders? Research traditions and theories relevant to this study are reviewed with the goal to consider theories which might be useful but are not obviously helpful at first glance, e.g. domestication research. Next, the concept of customer satisfaction in general is investigated. The following sub-chapter "Human-Computer Interaction" consists of a review of relevant approaches to explain satisfaction (or usage, acceptance), e.g. the well-known Technology Acceptance Model (TAM) or the concept of Flow. Finally, user interface design aspects and system evaluation methods are discussed.

In chapter three the conceptual model is developed which is the main focus of the study. Each of the dimensions hypothesised to have an influence on satisfaction with personalised internet applications is outlined.

Chapter four presents the study methodology used to identify the degree of influence each of the hypothesised factors has on satisfaction with personalised internet applications. The operationalisation of the respective constructs is described and how the survey instrument was developed. The internet applications used to validate the model are briefly delineated. Finally, the approach how study participants were encouraged to participate in the user survey is outlined.

Chapter five focuses on the results starting with the descriptive analyses and moving on to structural equation modelling. First, an overview of the demographic distribution of the sample is given. Second, the study participants are classified according to personal characteristics such as attitude towards online information search or internet familiarity. Finally, the participating personalised internet applications are compared in terms of the results they achieved when study participants evaluated them. The structural equation modelling part of the dissertation covers general issues such as model fit and the distinction between measurement and structural model. Next, results for an overall structural model as well as for multiple group analyses are presented. The final part of chapter five deals with results of expert interviews conducted to give additional insights and an outlook for future possible developments.

The final chapter six provides a conclusion of the main results and a discussion of the findings. Limitations of the study are outlined and implications for future research as well as for practitioners are given.

2 STATE OF THE FIELD – THEORETICAL BACKGROUND

This chapter starts from the most general topics which do play a role for this study and is narrowed down to the more specific issues. First, some definition and classification for personalised internet applications is introduced. Research traditions relevant to the field of usability, the adoption of and satisfaction with information systems are reviewed. Section 2.3 includes an overview of general theories about customer satisfaction. Next, theories about human computer interaction (HCI) are meta-analysed and the most prominent models (i.e. the TAM, contributions to Flow) are explained in greater detail. In Section 2.5 user interface design approaches will be discussed. The goal is to give a brief overview which design approaches exist to provide effective website design. Another relevant area for this study is usability testing and system evaluation, which will be dealt with in the final section of this chapter.

This chapter intends to give a quite widespread outline about existing theories relevant to the topic of personalised system and recommender evaluation.

The goals are:

- ⇨ to give a classification of personalised internet applications (PIA) on which is the focus of this research but also to give a definition of related systems such as recommenders,
- ⇨ to identify relevant research traditions of different disciplines and theories coming from satisfaction research,
- ⇨ to avoid missing important and relevant contributions, and
- ⇨ to adapt models or borrow concepts from other disciplines to the HCI and system evaluation topic.

2.1 Classification of Personalised Internet Applications

Personalised internet applications are the focus of this study. Therefore, this section is intended to give a classification and definition of personalisation and related terms such as adaptation, customisation, individualisation and recommendation. Furthermore, decision support systems (DSS) which can be seen as ancestors of personalised systems will be outlined as well.

According to Wright (2002) there are two types of personalisation. The first one allows the user to adapt the Graphical User Interface (GUI) to his or her own preferences. The second is concerned with the content of the system. The content is customised to the individual personal preferences of the user. Perugini and Ramakrishnan (2002) defined personalisation as the automatic adaptation of information content, structure or presentation to the preferences of the individual user. Similarly, Blom (2002) and Perugini & Ramakrishnan (2002) classified personalisation as a process that increases individual relevance by changing the content, structure, functionality, presentation (interface) or distinctiveness of a system. Adomavicius and Tuzhilin (2005a) named as examples of possible personalisation strategies: personalised content (pages or links), product and service recommendations or personalised information services.

What is the major goal and motivation to develop and use personalised internet applications? First of all, the amount of information provided on the Internet is uncountable. Often, consumers are lost in the plethora of the Internet. Therefore, efficient information search is simply a necessity. Search engines are one way to overcome these problems. However, they do not present the information in a personalised or customised way. Further support tools are needed to satisfy this need. Recommender or personalised systems are appropriate tools to present individualised information (Wei, Moreau, & Jennings, 2003). Moreover, there is a rising diversity of user needs (Lekakos & Giaglis, 2005). Thus, a personalised web site becomes more responsive to the unique and individual user's needs and preferences (Cingil, Dogac, & Azgin, 2000). The process of personalisation can be either system or user initiated (Blom, 2000, 2002). Kumar (2005) gave an overview of different personalisation techniques (see Figure 1).

The collection of user information can be done either implicitly or explicitly. While explicit profiling collects information or preferences of the user by directly asking him / her (e.g. to give some product ratings), implicit data collection tracks the user behaviour (Kumar, 2005). As far as the personalisation techniques are concerned there are several techniques. Simple filtering applies clustering of users. Members of similar groups get similar proposals (Kumar, 2005). Content based filtering (also called feature based filtering) methods personalise according to the attributes of a product or service which fit best to the current or past user's preferences (Adomavicius & Tuzhilin, 2005a; Wright, 2002). Personalisation is therefore based on the attributes of the item

(Adomavicius & Tuzhilin, 2005a; Runte, 2000; Wright, 2002). Adomavicius and Tuzhilin (2002) proposed an infomediary (a service that provides specialised information) called e-Butler. E-Butler enables personalised online shopping and takes preferences of the respective user into account and relates them to the attributes and characteristics of the products.

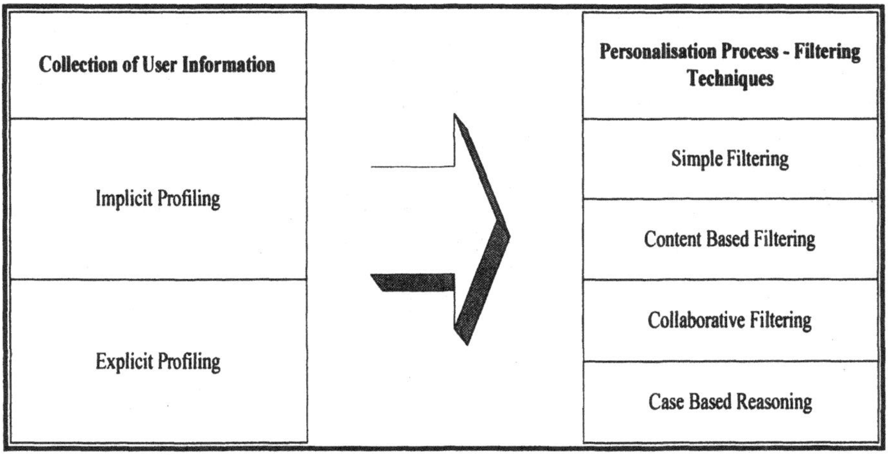

Figure 1. Personalisation Techniques
(adapted from Kumar, 2005)

The more advanced techniques to provide personalised and recommendation services consist of three major categories: Collaborative Filtering (CF), Case Based Reasoning (CBR) or hybrid approaches (Adomavicius & Tuzhilin, 2005b). Collaborative Filtering is considered to be the most successful recommendation or personalisation technique (Cho, Kim, & Kim, 2002; Ha, 2002). CF is defined as a technique using the behaviour of others when giving recommendations; it mimics word-of-mouth recommendations (Ansari, Essegaier, & Kohli, 2000; Pemberton, Rodden, & Procter, 2000). Recommendations are derived by the ratings of other similar users and of ratings in the past. Amazon is a very popular example using this technique. Case-Based Reasoning can be compared to human memory; previously experienced cases (concrete problem situations) are reused to solve new, similar cases. Furthermore, those cases are retained and the system is learning by each new problem (Aamodt & Plaza, 1994).

However, personalisation and recommendation methods are a well researched area applying also novel approaches, e.g. natural language processing (Berger, Dittenbach, & Merkl, 2004) or adaptive neural networks (Wallace, Maglongiannis, Karpouzis, Korzmentas, & Kollias, 2004). Often hybrid approaches are used by combining two of the above mentioned technologies, e.g. a content based approach together with collaborative filtering (Wright, 2002).

The terms adaptive, individualised or customised systems are used frequently as well. Therefore, some clarification will be made if these terms can be used synonymously to personalisation or if they have different meanings. Literature review shows that when considering adaptive systems they are often mentioned together with personalised systems (e.g. Liu, Wong, & Hui, 2003; Perkowitz & Etzioni, 2000). Systems using automatic personalisation have also been called "self-customising software" (Hirsh, Basu, & Davison, 2000). According to Ansari and Mela (2003), e-customisation is the process of adapting the content automatically for individual users. Finally, individualised content is often referred to as a technique for personalisation (Greer & Murtaza, 2003).

When speaking of personalised systems often the term recommendation system (also called simply recommender, advisory system or counselling system) comes up. Recommending items is often included when a personalisation process is performed because it helps to tailor the web site to the preferences and wishes of the user (Ha, 2002). Lekakos and Giaglis (2005) argue that recommenders are a special type of personalised systems. Groß and Sadeghi (2001) gave a general definition of recommenders proposing that such systems like chat rooms or forums offer advice from like-minded people. Applied to the context of e-commerce it is a relationship between a client and a server. The benefits of the latter would be for the e-commerce supplier or provider the increased probability to turn browsers into buyers, to enable cross-selling and finally, to enhance loyalty. The advantages for the user of such systems would be to get better results by being provided with product ratings and by having greater potential knowledge because of other users. The limitation to overcome is to guarantee a certain level of privacy (although it is rather difficult to get the right balance between personalisation and privacy).

According to Stohr and Viswanathan (1999) recommendation systems are a sub-category of decision support systems helping us to deal with the information overflow which leads to the next relevant group of systems: decision support systems. Research on decision support systems has already been conducted for a considerable amount of time having its origins in investigating management decision support systems and marketing decision support systems (MDSS), e.g. Wöber and Gretzel (2000). Furthermore, marketing and management support systems (e.g. Wierenga & van Bruggen 2000) or management information systems (MIS) are found as well in that context. O'Keefe and McEachern (1998) argued in their contribution about Web-based customer decision support systems (CDSS) that a consumer decision process can be split into five steps (see Figure 2).

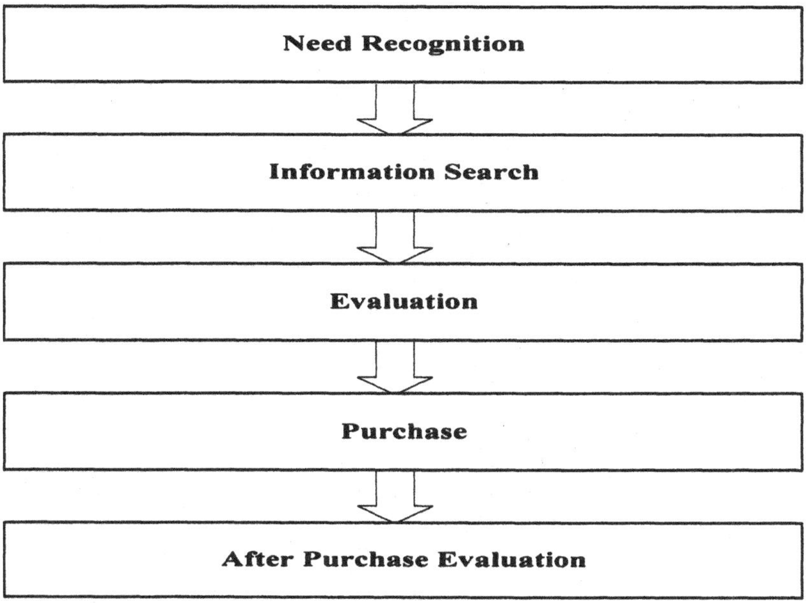

Figure 2. The Consumer Decision Making Process (O'Keefe & McEachern, 1998)

When considering which steps of the consumer decision making process are relevant to personalised systems, it is obvious that a personalised system should help in information search, evaluation and probably in the purchase phase (by providing appropriate ordering forms and payment systems) as well. Additionally, after purchase evaluation is provided by some personalised systems by offering rating tools for customers having already experienced the product or service. Finally, need recognition could also be pursued by offering personalised systems. The system can suggest products or services of which the user was not aware before but corresponds to his/her tastes and preferences.

2.2 Relevant Research Traditions and Theories

Various disciplines are of importance for this field of research: psychology, business (marketing and consumer behaviour), mass communication with uses and gratification research, adoption studies in information systems research and finally sociology contributing with domestication research.

Psychology comes first to one's mind when thinking about (user) behaviour. Especially social psychology plays a crucial role when searching for a theoretical foundation for behaviour. The theory of planned behaviour (TPB, Ajzen 1991) which originates from the Theory of Reasoned Action, TRA (Fishbein & Ajzen, 1975), is a well-known example often used in consumer behaviour research and serving as basis to develop user behaviour models (e.g. the TAM). Social Cognitive Theory (SCT) or Social Learning Theory (SLT) is a further relevant theory for this study. SCT is widely accepted for explaining behaviour, e.g. by incorporating the factor self-efficacy in a research model (Chan & Lu, 2004). The domain of cognitive absorption (e.g. Agarwal and Karahanna, 2000) and the notion of Flow (originally introduced by Csikszentmihalyi (1975) and adopted by Hoffman and Novak (1996) to the web context) play an important role as well. The hygiene and motivation theory originally published by Herzberg et al., (1967) was adapted by Zhang and Dran (2000) for website design and evaluation. The main assertion is that there are some basic factors or criteria (i.e. prerequisites) which have to be met otherwise dissatisfaction is caused. The latter, motivation factors, don't have to be met necessarily but if they are fulfilled they are likely to produce satisfaction. The motivational model (MM), with the core constructs of extrinsic and intrinsic motivation is well studied in different areas e.g. human resource management and is used to explain online behaviour as well (e.g. Shang et al., 2005).

Diffusion research is another relevant discipline applied in marketing or consumer research but also in sociology, education or anthropology. The focus is on the adoption and diffusion of innovations. Innovation diffusion theory (IDT) was proposed by Rogers (1976; 1995) and was defined as "the process by which innovation is communicated through certain channels among the members of a social system". IDT is often used as a basis in studies about new information technology. Thus, the relevance for the Internet is obvious. While obtaining information via the WWW is quite common nowadays, buying products and services online is still not that widespread. Diffusion of innovation theories serve as a basis to explore online buyer behaviour in general (e.g. Chen, Lee et al. 2004) or to investigate specific applications such as buying cars online (Molesworth & Suortti, 2001). IDT is applied in the m-commerce environment as well (e.g. Kauffman and Techatassanasoontorn 2005; Wu and Wang 2005).

Uses and gratifications research stemming from the area of mass communication have relevance for the Internet as well. Models of consumer motivations for media usage are provided including Internet usage. Katerattanakul (2002) suggests that consumers are looking for three main gratifications when using the Web: information search, consumer transactions and enjoyment. Eighmey and McCord (1998) concluded that in order for a computer-mediated form of communication to be chosen the first time, it needs to be entertaining and to offer exploration.

Obviously, in information systems research many contributions can be found about website adoption or satisfaction. Various journals are targeted at this research tradition: MIS Quarterly, Decision Support Systems, International Journal of Human-Computer Studies, Information Systems Research, to name but a few. Adoption research deals with all kinds of applications, e.g. automated teller machines (Dos Santos & Peffers, 1998) or computers (Venkatesh & Brown, 2001). A lot of lessons can be learned from research about the adoption of management information systems (MIS) and the adoption of decision support systems (DSS) or executive information systems (EIS).

The final research tradition, domestication research coming from sociology, anthropology or ethnology, studies the process of how a specific good, e.g. a car, a computer or a specific technology becomes part of people's lives (Anderson, 2003; Pedersen & Ling, 2003). Originally, the term "domestication" was applied to the use of quite new products or technologies in home life. Often "domestication" is used in a wider context and means the general use of a specific product or technology (Habib, 2003). Especially in the field of ICTs, a number of domestication studies were realised, e.g. Stewart (2003), Anderson (2003), Habib and Cornford (2001).

Obviously, various research disciplines play an important role when looking for models explaining system usage or satisfaction. Next, customer satisfaction in general will be discussed. Afterwards selected models of human-computer interaction (HCI) stemming from the above named research traditions are introduced.

2.3 Customer Satisfaction in General

General theories about customer satisfaction and the assessment of services will be discussed to give an overview of what affects customer behaviour. Some of the approaches will be found again in later chapters because they are of relevance to satisfaction with personalised internet applications as well.

Vavra (1997) introduced a model of the satisfaction process depending on expectations, perceived performance, prior experience, ease of evaluating and desires. Prior experience is determined by a lot of antecedent influencers such as demographics, word of mouth, and nature of competition. Expectations are affected by desires and prior experience. Perceived performance is influenced by the ease of evaluating and prior experience. The mediator variable is confirmation / disconfirmation being directly affected by expectations, perceived performance and prior experience. According to Novak, Hoffman et al. (2000), there are a lot of factors influencing behaviour such as involvement, knowledge, emotions, motives, attitudes, values, personality, the type of information acquisition and the kind of processing of information.

Parasuraman et al. (1988) described a model of five dimensions of service quality (SERVQUAL): tangibles, reliability, responsiveness, assurance and empathy. Although the model was originally constructed for the traditional service sector it can be well adapted to computer-mediated environments, tangibles meaning the Graphical User Interface (GUI), reliability can be the error probability of the system itself or the trustworthiness of the information and/or recommendations given. Responsiveness can be related to the fact that a personalised internet application (PIA) should be a highly interactive and conversational one. Assurance is another aspect named by Parasumaran et al., which can be translated into the PIA context to the extent that a system is capable to give appropriate recommendations. Prerequisites to give appropriate proposals are e.g. a large knowledge base and intelligent recommendation functions. Another aspect of assurance is that the system is able to convince the user about the goodness of the suggestions or recommendations. Finally, empathy in the context of recommender systems can be the degree to which the system is able to respond to the wishes and preferences stated by the user.

In 2000, Zeithaml et al. introduced a framework of e-service quality including further dimensions (additionally to the five dimensions named in connection with the SERVQUAL model: access, flexibility, ease of navigation, efficiency, trust (added to assurance), security/privacy, price knowledge, site aesthetics and customization/personalization. Wang and Tang (2003) used the SERVQUAL model as starting point and developed an EC-SERVQUAL model containing four dimensions: reliability, responsiveness, assurance and empathy. Loiacono et al. (2000) proposed a WebQual instrument measuring 12 dimensions divided into 4 umbrella terms: usefulness (dimensions: informational fit-to-task, tailored communications, trust, response time), ease of use (ease of understanding, intuitive operations), entertainment (visual appeal, innovativeness, emotional appeal) and finally, complimentary relationship (consistent image, on-line completeness, relative advantage). Another WebQual approach was introduced by Barnes and Vidgen (2001). The authors developed their instrument over time and therefore, several variants of WebQual exist. WebQual version 2.0 included 10 dimensions (aesthetics, understanding the individual, communication, access, security, credibility, navigation, competence, responsiveness and reliability). Their latest WebQual version 4.0 (Barnes & Vidgen, 2003) is reduced to a quite parsimonious model of four dimensions: usability, design, information and service.

In 2005 Parasuraman et al. proposed an E-S-QUAL (electronic service quality) scale consisting of four dimensions based on SERVQUAL: efficiency, fulfilment, system availability, and privacy. Additionally, they introduced a second scale called E-RecS-QUAL which is intended to be used when nonroutine incidents happen with the web sites. Three constructs are covered by E-RecS-QUAL (e-recovery service quality scale): responsiveness, compensation and contact (Parasuraman et al., 2005).

Servicescapes is another approach which was originally proposed for service organizations (Bitner, 1992) and later applied to the Web context (Galan & Gonzalez, 2001; Zins, 2002). Servicescapes studies the impact of physical surroundings on consumption settings. Environmental dimensions, i.e. ambient conditions, space/function, signs, symbols and artefacts do have an influence on the holistic environment (the perceived servicescapes), on the internal response of the consumers and the employees and finally, on their behaviour. The Webscape model of Galan and Gonzalez (2001) uses a similar framework but adapted to website design. The environment/"creative palette" (e.g. colours, layout) of a website influences the holistic environment (consisting of four main factors: informational dimension, entertainment, interactivity and effectiveness dimension). The holistic environment (and the moderating effects) finally influences responses. A different Webscape model was proposed by Zins (2002). In his framework, factors influencing response are classified according to content, control and process characteristics. Content characteristics refer to the type of source, the scope of content, interactivity and vividness. Control characteristics include challenges (time pressure, task complexity), skills and decision style. Finally, process characteristics, i.e. decision rules and decision process have an influence on the response. While the first, servicescapes, measure the influencing factors on consumer and employee responses the Webscape model concentrates on consumer responses.

2.4 Human-Computer Interaction (HCI)

The intention of this chapter is to give an overview of models, theories and concepts explaining user behaviour in computer-mediated environments (CME) and human computer-interaction (HCI). Numerous approaches examining HCI, user acceptance, satisfaction, information systems' (IS) success and their influencing factors, exist. Models and concepts which concentrate on HCI and CME will now be used to review factors which mostly influence the usage of and/or satisfaction with a system. HCI is a well studied topic and a large number of contributions can be found. Theories are meta-analysed and the most prominent models (i.e. the TAM, Flow theory) are explained in greater detail. The goal is to give an overview which approaches provide suggestions to better design or improve a website. Which are the criteria influencing user satisfaction or usage of a system? A prerequisite to design or evaluate information systems is to know about these crucial factors.

The basic goal of the HCI endeavour is to design, construct and evaluate computer-based systems and therefore, enable an efficient and satisfactory use (Hartson, 1998). HCI comprises the design, evaluation and implementation of information systems and their interaction with users (Hewett et al., 1996). The attempts of this discipline are to increase safety, utility, effectiveness, efficiency, accessibility, and usability for users of those interactive systems (Stephanidis, 2001). The question is which are the influencing factors determining computer usage and satisfaction? Therefore, a brief review of existing concepts explaining HCI seems helpful. In the sub-sections following, the most prominent approaches are illustrated in greater detail. An overview of HCI approaches will be given which is by no means an exhaustive list of all contributions.

2.4.1 The Technology Acceptance Model (TAM)

The Technology Acceptance Model (TAM) introduced by Davis (1989) is a widely known and often tested model to explain the acceptance with an information system or web site. Originally, the TAM stems from the theory of planned behaviour (TPB) which in turn was amended from the theory of reasoned action (TRA). The TRA (Fishbein & Ajzen, 1975) and subsequently the TPB (Ajzen, 1991) are theories often applied to explain human behaviour and also HCI. Figure 3 outlines the components of the TRA.

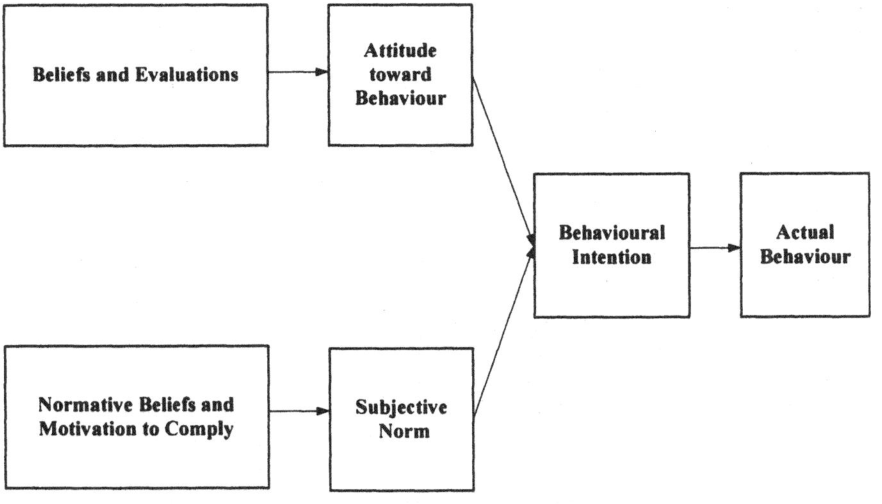

Figure 3. The Theory of Reasoned Action (TRA; Fishbein and Ajzen 1975)

The TRA comes from the discipline of psychology and postulates that behaviour and behavioural intention is influenced by attitude and subjective norm (i.e. social norms). Both of them are in turn determined by beliefs and evaluations as well as by normative beliefs and motivation to comply. Beliefs are defined as a person's subjective probability judgements, how the person sees herself / himself and the environment. Those beliefs will result in some outcomes which will be evaluated (Fishbein & Ajzen, 1975). "Normative beliefs and motivation to comply" deals with the expectations of referent groups or referent individuals and the person's motivation to fulfil these expectations. Subjective norm describes the behaviour which is performed because of social pressure (Ajzen, 1991). In 1991, Ajzen extended the TRA by perceived behavioural control which is influenced by control beliefs. Additionally, he points out the influences among the respective constructs (see Figure 4).

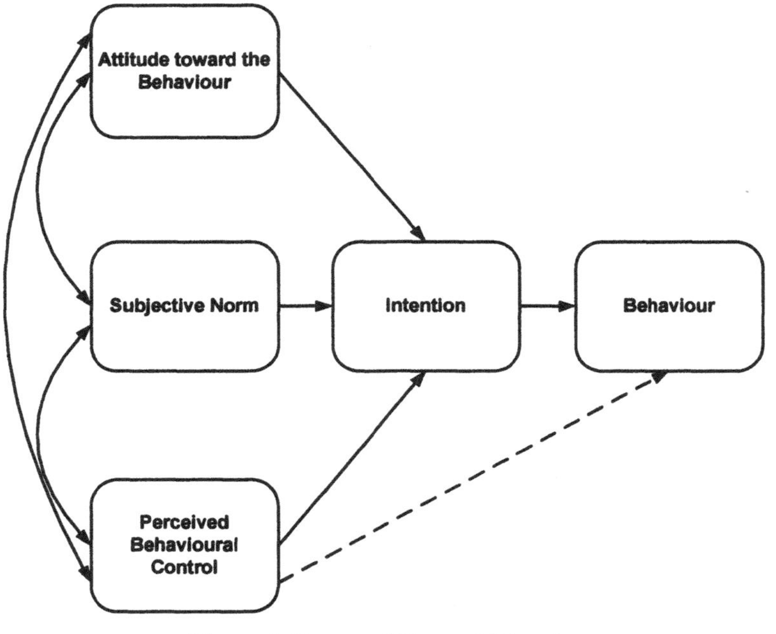

Figure 4. Theory of Planned Behaviour (TPB; Ajzen, 1991)

Perceived behavioural control is defined as the person's perceived ability to perform certain behaviour. This construct is determined by control beliefs which can be defined as supporting or hampering influences to perform that desired behaviour (Ajzen, 1991).

On the basis of the TRA Davis proposed the Technology Acceptance Model (TAM) in 1989. Meanwhile, TAM has become a well-researched and often confirmed model. The TAM relies on two factors explaining human behaviour when using a system: perceived usefulness and perceived ease of use. Perceived usefulness describes the user's point of view of enhancing his or her performance by using the system. Perceived ease of use is the degree of effort the user believes he or she will need for using a particular system (Davis, Bagozzi et al. 1989). The TAM is shown in Figure 5.

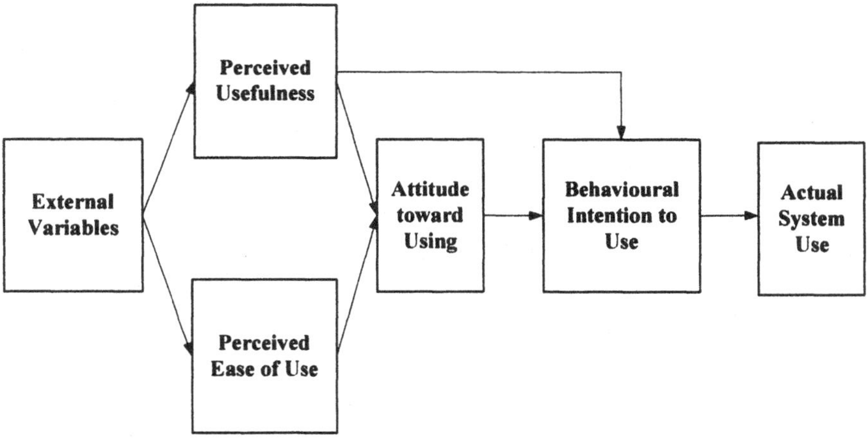

Figure 5. The original Technology Acceptance Model (Davis, 1989)

TAM was supported by several studies, e.g. Lederer et al. (2000) tested the TAM in the WWW context and their results confirmed the TAM. Venkatesh and Davis extended the TAM (and named it TAM2) in 2000 and added subjective norm, image, output quality, result demonstrability and job relevance as further influencing factors. However, Legris et al. (2003), reviewed several TAM contributions and confirmed the model with the explicit constraint that human social change processes have to be included in a broader model. Furthermore, they argued that TAM and TAM2 only explain about 40% of system's use (Legris et al., 2003). Therefore, numerous studies can be found in the literature extending the original TAM model. They add various factors to the previously named perceived usefulness and ease of use. Examples are perceived accessibility and the customer's attitude towards the Web (Jeong & Lambert, 2001), perceived playfulness (Moon & Kim, 2001), application-specific self efficacy (Yi & Hwang, 2003) or trust and perceived risk (Pavlou, 2001). Wöber, Scharl et al. (2002) introduced a framework distinguishing three categories of factors influencing perceived usefulness and perceived ease of use, i.e. personal factors (expectations and experience), system factors (such as product, speed, intelligence and services) and media factors (speed and operability). Personal and media factors are uncontrollable by the system and the management whereas system factors represent controllable criteria.

Table 1 gives a short overview of selected TAM-related contributions but is by no means exhaustive since there are numerous contributions in this field of research. The table not only indicates different approaches and their author/s but also distinguishes between the independent variables (influencing factors) and the dependent variables (which factor/s is the model explaining, e.g. user satisfaction) for each approach. Table 1 does not always include the antecedents for the independent variables as it is intended to give just an overview and in some studies a lot of antecedents were analysed. This is also true for the subsequent tables in this sub-section.

Table 1. Selected TAM-Related Contributions

Author/s and Publication Year	Article title	Independent (Influencing) Variables	Dependent Variable (Outcome)
Childers, T.L., Carr, C.L., Peck, J. and S. Carson (2001)	Hedonic and Utilitarian Motivations for Online Retail Shopping Behaviour	Usefulness, Ease of Use, Enjoyment	Attitude
Davis, F.D. (1989)	Perceived Usefulness, Perceived Ease of Use, and User Acceptance of Information Technology	Perceived Usefulness, Perceived Ease of Use	(Attitude toward Using => Behavioural Intention to Use =>) Actual System Use

Author/s and Publication Year	**Article title**	**Independent (Influencing) Variables**	**Dependent Variable (Outcome)**
Davis, F.D., Bagozzi, R.P. and P.R. Warshaw (1989)	User Acceptance of Computer Technology: A Comparison of Two Theoretical Models	Perceived Usefulness, Perceived Ease of Use	(Attitude toward Using => Behavioural Intention to Use =>) Actual System Use
Jeong, M. and C.U. Lambert (2001)	Adaptation of an Information Quality Framework to Measure Customers' Behavioural Intentions to Use Lodging Web Sites	Perceived Usefulness, Perceived Ease of Use, Perceived Accessibility, Attitudes	Intention to Use Information, Information Use => Recommen-dation
Kucuk and Arslan (2000)	A Cross Cultural Comparison of Consumers' Acceptance of the Web Marketing Facilities	Ease of Use, Usefulness	(Attitude and Intention =>) Acceptance (of Web Marketing Facilities)
Moon, J.-W. and Y.-G. Kim (2001)	Extending the TAM for a World-Wide-Web Context	Perceived Usefulness, Perceived Ease of Use, Perceived Playfulness	(Attitude toward Using => Behavioural Intention to Use =>) Actual Usage
Morosan, C. and M. Jeong (2006)	Understanding Travelers' Adoption of Hotel Reservation Web Sites	Perceived Usefulness, Perceived Ease of Use, Perceived Playfulness	Attitudes => Intentions

Author/s and Publication Year	**Article title**	**Independent (Influencing) Variables**	**Dependent Variable (Outcome)**
Pavlou, P.A. (2001)	Consumer Intentions to Adopt Electronic Commerce – Incorporating Trust and Risk in the TAM	Perceived Usefulness, Perceived Ease of Use, Trust, Perceived Risk	Intention to Transact Online
Shang, R.-A., Chen, Y.-C. and L. Shen (2005)	Extrinsic Versus Intrinsic Motivations for Consumers to Shop On-line	Perceived Usefulness, Perceived Ease of Use, Fashion Involvement, Cognitive Absorption	Shopping Online
Teo, T.S., Lim, V.K. and R.Y. Lai (1999)	Intrinsic and Extrinsic Motivation in Internet Usage	Perceived Enjoyment, Perceived Usefulness, Perceived Ease of Use	Internet Usage
Yi, M. Y. and Y. Hwang (2003)	Predicting the Use of Web-based Information Systems: Self-efficacy, Enjoyment, Learning Goal Orientation, and the Technology Acceptance Model	Usefulness, Ease of Use, Application Specific Self-Efficacy	Behavioural Intention => Use
Van der Heijden, H. (2004)	User Acceptance of Hedonic Information Systems	Perceived Enjoyment, Perceived Usefulness, Perceived Ease of Use	Intention to Use

Author/s and Publication Year	Article title	Independent (Influencing) Variables	Dependent Variable (Outcome)
Venkatesh V. and F.D. Davis (2000)	A Theoretical Extension of the Technology Acceptance Model: Four Longitudinal Field Studies	Perceived Usefulness, Perceived Ease of Use, Subjective Norm	Intention to Use => Usage Behaviour

A number of criteria could influence perceived usefulness and perceived ease of use. An illustration which factors could determine both factors is given by Figure 6. Some factors such as navigation, interactivity, services can be influenced by the system whereas others cannot or can hardly be influenced by the system and its provider, i.e. expectations, experience or the connection speed of the user.

Furthermore, models can be found which are similar to TAM but the constructs are named differently, e.g. the IS success model (DeLone and McLean 1992) which forms the basis of the next sub-section.

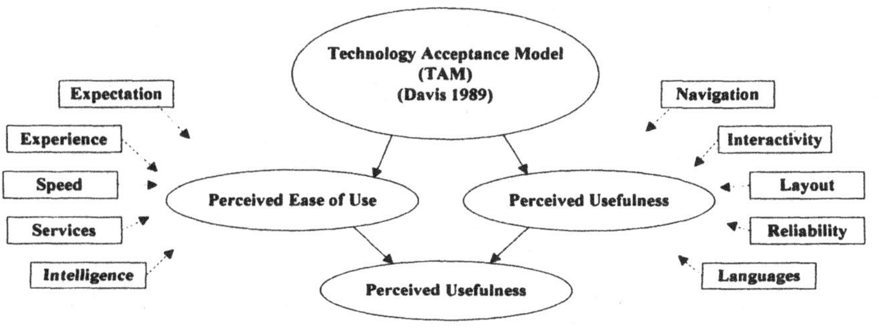

Figure 6. TAM and Possible Influencing Factors (adapted from Davis 1989)

2.4.2 The IS Success Model

The IS Success Model originally proposed by DeLone and McLean (1992) included two major dimensions (system quality and information quality) to explain use and user satisfaction (these two further influence the individual and organisational impact). System quality is concerned with the information processing itself whereas information quality means basically the content. These two dimensions are very similar to ease of use and usefulness. Later, DeLone and McLean (2002) added service quality to the IS Success Model. They adapted service quality from the SERVQUAL measurement instrument (Parasuraman et al., 1988). Three factors (responsiveness, assurance and empathy) were included under the overall term of service quality. Negash et al. (2003) used the same combination of independent variables but added the factor "tangible reliability" such as a modern looking interface, appealing material or dependability to the construct service quality. Lee and Kozar (2005) added the construct vendor-specific quality. Vendor-specific quality comprises the vendor's awareness, reputation and price competitiveness. Table 2 gives an overview of the original IS Success contributions as well as of extension and confirmation studies.

Table 2. Selected IS Success Model-Related Contributions

Author/s and Publication Year	**Article title**	**Independent (Influencing) Variables**	**Dependent Variable (Outcome)**
DeLone, W.H. and E.R. McLean (1992)	Information Systems Success: the Quest for the Dependent Variable	System Quality, Information Quality	Use, User Satisfaction => Individual Impact => Organizational Impact
DeLone, W.H. and E.R. McLean (2003)	The DeLone and McLean Model of Information Systems Success: A Ten-Year Update	System Quality, Information Quality, Service Quality	Use (Intention to Use), User Satisfaction => Net Benefits

Author/s and Publication Year	**Article title**	**Independent (Influencing) Variables**	**Dependent Variable (Outcome)**
Lee, Y. and K. A. Kozar (2005)	Investigating the Effect of Website Quality on E-Business Success: An Analytic Hierarchy Process (AHP) Approach	Information, System, Service and Vendor-Specific Quality	Choice of the Most Preferred Website
McGill, T., Hobbs, V. and J. Klobas (2003)	User-Developed Applications and Informations Systems Success: A Test of DeLone and McLean's Model	System Quality, Information Quality	User Satisfaction => Intended Use and Perceived Individual Impact => Organizational Impact
Negash, S., Ryan, T. and M. Igbaria (2003)	Quality and Effectiveness in Web-based Customer Support Systems	Information, System and Service Quality	Effectiveness (User Satisfaction)
Rodgers, W., Negash, S. and K. Suk (2005)	The Moderating Effect of On-line Experience on the Antecedents and Consequences of On-line Satisfaction	Information, System and Service Quality	On-line Satisfaction, On-line Loyalty
Stockdale, R. and M. Borovicka (2006)	Using Quality Dimensions in the Evaluation of Websites	Information, System and Service Quality	None (was an evaluation instrument development)

2.4.3 Flow

Another concept dealing with human-computer interaction is Flow. Originally, the term "Flow" comes from psychology and was introduced by Csikszentmihalyi in 1975. Often Flow was validated in a sports context like kayaking e.g. Jones, et al. (2000). Csikszentmihalyi (1975) tested Flow when playing chess, dancing, climbing rocks, or even working. However, Flow can be found experiencing almost every activity including surfing the WWW (King, 2003). Hoffman and Novak (1996) and Novak, Hoffman and Yung (2000) adapted Flow to the web context. They tested Flow and its constructs on a general level meaning no specific web sites were involved.

Flow is described as a state of mind where the user is completely devoted to the use of a system and forgets everything else around him or her, like time. Thus, the aim is to create a compelling online experience to facilitate Flow. An important condition to make Flow possible is that the person's perceived skills match the person's perceived challenge (Csikszentmihalyi, 1975; Hoffman & Novak, 1996; King, 2003). If a state of boredom or anxiety occurs Flow cannot be experienced.

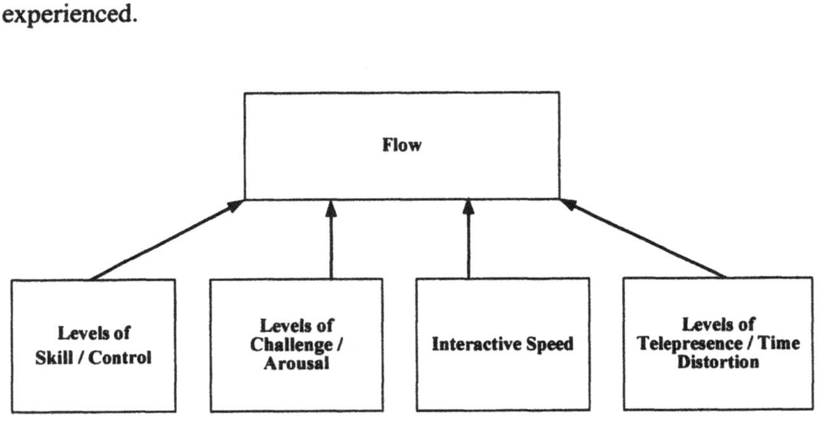

Figure 7. Flow and its Direct Influences in CME (Novak et al., 2000)

Figure 7 illustrates the direct influences determining the cognitive state of Flow. The ultimate goal to achieve is not Flow but differs according to the area of application, e.g. shopping behaviour (Smith & Sivakumar, 2004), intention to purchase (Korzaan, 2003), positive affect and exploratory behaviour (Hoffman &

Novak, 1996) and furthermore, a compelling customer experience in the online environment (Hoffman & Novak, 1996; Novak, Hoffman, & Yung, 2000).

Skill was defined by Novak et al. (2000) as the user's capacity to act during online navigation. However, Skadberg and Kimmel (2004) had a different view about "skill" in their study about Flow on the web. They defined it as the user's knowledge about the web site's topic. Control refers to two aspects (Novak et al., 2000). First, how is the user's perceived ability to navigate on the web site? How is the web site responding to inputs?

Challenge was defined by Hoffman and Novak (1996) as the user's available possibilities of action and arousal being the "theoretical correlate of challenge" (Novak et al., 2000). The interactive speed deals with questions such as the loading time of the web site or the computer's response time (Novak et al., 2000).

Telepresence is the mediated perception of the environment (Steuer, 1992). According to Steuer (1992) the user perceives two environments. The first one is the physical one and the second is the CME. A person not only perceives the real environment when surfing a site but also the virtual environment (Skadberg & Kimmel, 2004). Telepresence occurs when the virtual environment is perceived as more dominant or real than the actual physical (Novak et al., 2000). Time distortion was operationalised by "loosing track of time" and "time goes by quickly" by Novak, et al. (2000).

Indirect influences on Flow are importance to the user (i.e. involvement, intrinsic interest), focused attention, interactive speed and the experience a person has using the Internet (Novak et al., 2000). Focused attention was defined by Csikszentmihalyi (1975) as the "centering of attention on a limited stimulus field". Operationalisation included questions concerning intent absorption or full concentration (Novak et al., 2000). Table 3 outlines selected approaches dealing with Flow.

Finneran and Zhang (2003) included flow in their so-called Person, Artifact, Task (PAT) Model. These three factors serve as flow antecedents. The person's characteristics are influenced by trait attributes (i.e. personality which is hard or impossible to change) and state attributes (e.g. mood) which is dynamic. Artefacts are the tools and in the case of the Internet the web site. The task is the specific goal a user wants to perform.

According to Hearst et al. (2002), browsing should be supported that the flow of interaction is not inhibited. The chain of thought should not be interrupted.

Such supporting features could be relevance feedback ("more like this") or query previews (to avoid empty or very few results) in the context of personalised internet applications.

Table 3. Selected Flow-related Approaches

Author/s and Publication Year	**Article title**	**Independent (Influencing) Variables**	**Dependent Variable (Outcome)**
Hoffman, T.P., and Novak D.L. (1996)	Marketing in Hypermedia Computer-Mediated Environments: Conceptual Foundations	Telepresence / Time Distortion, Focused Attention, Interactive Speed, Skill / Control, Challenge / Arousal	Flow (=> Positive Affect, Exploratory Behaviour)
Novak, T.P., Hoffman, D.L. and Y.-F. Yung (2000)	Measuring the Customer Experience in Online Environments: A Structural Modeling Approach	Skill / Control, Challenge / Arousal, Interactive Speed, Telepresence / Time Distortion	Flow
Finneran, C.M. and Zhang, P. (2003)	A Person-Artefact-Task (PAT) Model of Flow Antecedents in Computer-Mediated Environments	Person, Artifact, Task	Flow Experience => Flow Consequences

Author/s and Publication Year	Article title	Independent (Influencing) Variables	Dependent Variable (Outcome)
Skadberg and Kimmel (2004)	Visitors' Flow Experience While Browsing a Web Site: its Measurement, Contributing Factors and Consequences	Telepresence, Domain Knowledge / Skill, Information in the Web Site / Challenge	Optimal Flow Experience => Increased Learning => Changes of Attitude & Behaviour

Flow is undoubtedly an interesting and valuable contribution. However, doubts remain that the above named constructs like telepresence, the state of flow or focused attention can be measured reliably. Nevertheless, it is suggested that hedonic factors become more and more important. Therefore, additional endeavours considering hedonic influencing factors will be outlined in the following section.

2.4.4 Hedonic aspects

The importance of emotions is recognised more and more in the e-commerce world (e.g. Gonzáles, et al., 2002, Arnold and Reynolds, 2003). However, the importance of hedonic driven motivations is investigated in the field of consumer behaviour as well (e.g. Hirschman and Holbrook, 1982, McAlister and Pessemier, 1982). Therefore, a literature review of hedonic influences in a general consumer behaviour context is given followed by an overview of approaches integrating the hedonic dimension in web consumer behaviour.

2.4.4.1 General Consumer Behaviour Context

Hedonic-driven aspects of consumption and consumer behaviour were already considered as important influencing factors long before the satisfaction and acceptance research for information systems (IS) and web-based systems began.

Hirschman and Holbrook (1982) outlined that consumption and consumer behaviour is motivated by hedonic influences such as fantasy, emotive and multisensory aspects. Such factors could be tastes, sounds, scents, visual or tactile appeals. They argued that experiential aspects such as consumer fantasies, feelings and fun aspects should be considered as important variables in the consumption process (Holbrook & Hirschman, 1982). Laros and Steenkamp (2005) investigated emotions with their positive (i.e. contentment, happiness) and negative effects (i.e. anger, shame, fear, sadness) in the field of consumer behaviour.

Already in 1979, Zuckerman pointed out the concept of sensation seeking which he relates to entertainment, fashion or food. Raju (1980) investigated in his study the relationships between personality traits, exogenous variables (such as age, education), the arousal seeking tendency (optimum stimulation level) and in turn the exploratory tendencies. McAlister and Pessemier (1982) conducted an interdisciplinary review for the concept of variety seeking behaviour. Varied behaviour was defined as switching between alternatives: either products or services or activities. They found out that there are two basic schools: those saying that varied behaviour is not explicable or too complex to explain. The other school argues that there are two explanations for varied behaviour: either because of variation purposes themselves or because of some other motivation (McAlister & Pessemier, 1982).

Kroeber-Riel and Weinberg (1996) distinguished between affective and cognitive behaviour. According to them affect is a short-term feeling, emotion or reaction of acceptance or rejection. A cognitive process, on the other hand, is defined as rational thinking.

Spangenberg and Voss (1997) developed a scale measuring hedonic versus utilitarian dimensions of attitude. In 2003, Voss et al., conducted a study in which they worked out a parsimonious scale including five positive and negative statements for the hedonic and for the utilitarian scale (see Table 4).

Lynch and Srull (1982) found out that higher attention is captured by providing novel or unexpected information. They called it the phenomenon of selective attention. Bettman and Luce (1998) made an even stronger proposal by suggesting that consumers' attention is caught involuntarily if novel, unexpected, surprising or extremely salient information is presented.

Baumgartner and Steenkamp (1996) as well as Steenkamp and Burgess (2002) outlined in their studies the exploratory tendencies in consumer behaviour. The purposes of the consumer when pursuing exploratory shopping behaviour are for example to experience novel and exciting purchases, avoid boredom, satisfy curiosity or being innovative (Baumgartner & Steenkamp, 1996). They also developed a scale of exploratory buying behaviour tendencies (EBBT).

Table 4. Hedonic – Utilitarian Scale
(Voss et. al., 2003)

ITEMS			
UTILITARIAN		HEDONIC	
Effective	Ineffective	Not fun	Fun
Helpful	Unhelpful	Dull	Exciting
Functional	Not functional	Not delightful	Delightful
Necessary	Unnecessary	Not thrilling	Thrilling
Practical	Impractical	Enjoyable	Unenjoyable

A few examples were given of how emotional or variety-seeking factors are considered in consumer behaviour research. These ideas are increasingly applied for IS and web-based applications as well.

2.4.4.2 Online or Information Technology Context

Enjoyment, playfulness, fun, exploratory browsing behaviour – these are some attempts used to describe the hedonic component of a web site visit and an online recommendation process. Several studies (e.g. Moon and Kim, 2001, Teo, et al., 1999) investigated its influence and demonstrated the importance of these factors.

These hedonic components, the desire for exploration, the feeling of joy, pleasure, fun during the interaction with the website presents a certain kind of motivator factor. According to Zhang and Dran (2000) there are two types of web site factors: hygiene and motivator factors. The first make a web site functional and serviceable, these are factors absolutely necessary for a Web site. User dissatisfaction is very likely to be caused if these characteristics are not available on the respective sites. The latter ones are factors which are not necessary but which may create additional value and contribute to user satisfaction. In their study they found out that enjoyment, cognitive outcomes and visual appearance are (among others) so-called motivator factors (Zhang & Dran, 2000).

Van der Heijden and Sorensen (2003) applied an extended hedonic / utilitarian scale (HED/UT scale) to the context of mobile information service. Childers, et al. (2001) argued in their research about online retail shopping that a web site provider has to consider both aspects: hedonic and utilitarian drivers. The increasing importance of hedonic components requires establishing a so-called "Webmosphere" by design and interactive features.

According to Betts (2001) four types of online shopping visits can be distinguished:

- ⇨ Directed-purchase visits: the consumer buys right away.
- ⇨ Search and deliberation visits: the consumer is searching information about a product / service and intends to purchase.
- ⇨ Hedonic-browsing visits: shopping is done primarily for pleasure or recreation.
- ⇨ Knowledge-building visits: exploratory browsing is pursued to learn more about the marketplace which could influence long-term shopping behaviour.

Novak, et al. (2003) highlighted in their study about online consumption behaviour the distinction between goal- directed behaviour vs. experiential experiences (see Table 5). The definition of Novak, et al. (2003) is a broader one and goes beyond the concept of hedonic motivations which is just a part of the experiential behaviour. Furthermore, experiential behaviour could involve fun aspects, non-directed search or affective behaviour.

Table 5. Goal-directed and Experiential Online Behaviour (Novak et al., 2003)

Goal-Directed	**Experiental**
Extrinsic motivation	Intrinsic motivation
Instrumental orientation	Ritualized orientation
Situational involvement	Enduring involvement
Utilitarian benefits/value	Hedonic benefits/value
Directed (prepurchase) search	Nondirected (ongoing) search; browsing
Goal-directed choice	Navigational choice

Goal-Directed	Experiental
Cognitive	Affective
Work	Fun
Planned purchases; repurchasing	Compulsive shopping; impulse buys

Rodgers, et al. (2005) included in their measurement scale about information quality the dimension entertainment which they operationalised with entertaining, enjoyable, pleasing and fun to use.

Eroglu et al. (2003) emphasised the importance of online atmospheric cues which have an effect upon the user's emotional and cognitive states and in turn, influence the shopping outcome. Their model of Stimulus-Organism-Response is outlined in Figure 8. Richard (2005) investigated the influence of internet atmospherics on purchase intentions and included constructs such as exploratory behaviour, entertainment, but also navigational cues and structure in her research model.

When speaking of hedonic dimensions of web consumer behaviour the term "Exploratory Browsing Behaviour" arises. Exploratory Behaviour can be defined as browsing the web and visiting sites or links because of curiosity or variety-seeking (Korzaan, 2003). Huang (2000) explored online exploratory shopping behaviour and found out that novelty, contrasting, surprising and/or rare information, product or service, is a driving factor for the desire to explore a web site.

According to Mycoted (2004), a creativity and innovation company, three forms of browsing can be distinguished:

- ⇨ *Purposive browsing:* the user is looking for a specific pre-defined piece of information (utilitarian browsing behaviour, the goal is to find useful information)
- ⇨ *Capricious browsing:* information is randomly examined and there is no specific objective.
- ⇨ *Exploratory browsing:* inspiration is sought.

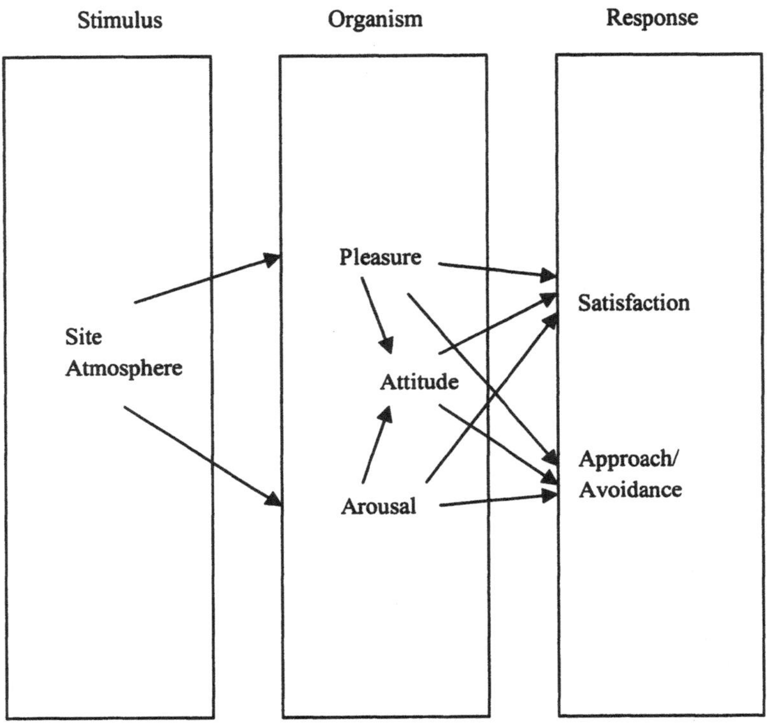

Figure 8. Pleasure and Arousal Components of a Stimulus Organism Response Model (Eroglu, et al., 2003)

Rowley (2002) differentiates further between intentional and unintentional browsing and controlled and uncontrolled browsing environments. Intentional browsing is described as additional information seeking due to insufficient information whereas unintentional browsing occurs if e.g. the search strategy was inappropriate. Controlled or uncontrolled browsing events could be facilitated by the web site provider – e.g. is the web site intended to encourage browsing proactively by features that attract attention or induce browsing (Rowley, 2002)?

According to Davis, Bagozzi and Warshaw (1992) and Moon and Kim (2001) the construct perceived enjoyment is the extent to which the activity of using the computer is perceived to be related to enjoyment and pleasure itself, apart from any performance consequences or extrinsic rewards. Van der Heijden (2004) added in his study about online user acceptance the construct perceived enjoyment to the TAM constructs perceived usefulness and perceived ease of use. The measurement of perceived enjoyment was affected by using four bipolar scales: enjoyable – disgusting, exciting – dull, pleasant – unpleasant, interesting – boring.

Similarly the concept of playfulness is understood to be one's belief that interacting with the WWW constitutes an intrinsic motivation factor and was found to have an influence on attitude, intentions and/or actual usage (Moon & Kim, 2001; Morosan & Jeong, 2006).

Cognitive Absorption (CA) is another popular concept dealing with intrinsic motivations of users. Shang, et al. (2005). used cognitive absorption as antecedent for perceived ease of use and usefulness as well as a direct influencer on online shopping behaviour. Saade and Bahli (2005) defined cognitive absorption as a state of deep involvement with the system. Such holistic experiences like enjoyment can be measured with the concept of CA. CA served as an antecedent for perceived ease of use and usefulness and had three dimensions in the study of Saade and Bahli: temporal dissociation, focused immersion and heightened enjoyment. Agarwal and Karahanna (2000) referred to CA as holistic experiences with technology and measured the construct with 5 dimensions. They applied control and curiosity additionally to the other three dimensions of Saade and Bahli.

When comparing the concept of CA to Flow some similarities arise. The dimensions of temporal dissociation and focused immersion of Agarwal and Karahanna (2000) and Saade and Bahli (2005) resemble time distortion and focused attention in the application of the concept of Flow of Hoffman and Novak (1996) and Novak, et al. (2000). Saade and Bahli included control which was considered by Hoffman and Novak (1996) and Novak, et al. (2000) as well.

The pending question is now: which buzzwords were mentioned in connection to online behaviour which is motivated hedonically? Figure 9 gives an idea of different concepts and models found but is not intended as an exhaustive enumeration. Furthermore, it is important to note that some of the constructs mentioned were used as antecedents by some studies whereas in others they served as direct influencers on the dependent variable, e.g. satisfaction or online behaviour.

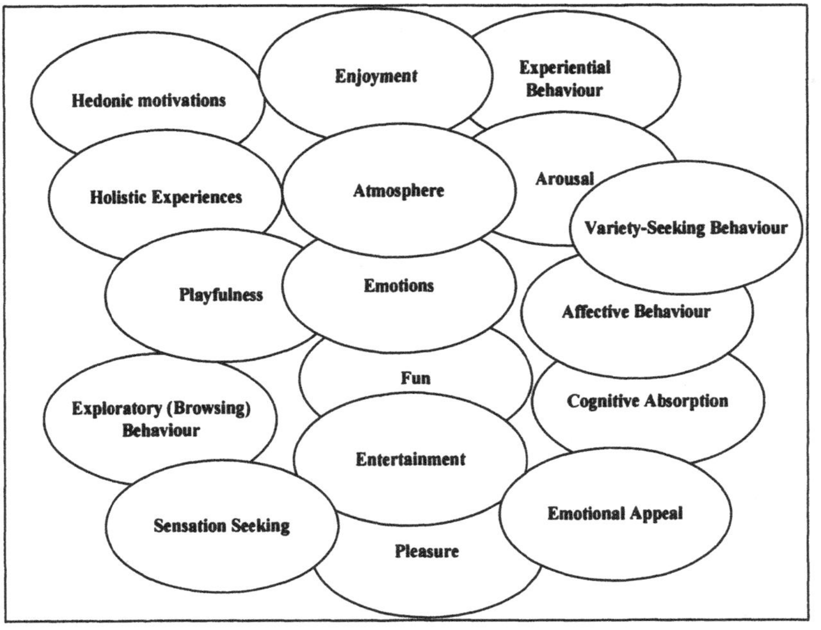

Figure 9. Concepts of Hedonic Motivated User Behaviour

2.4.5 Other Approaches

Apart from the models mentioned in further sub-sections, there are other endeavours having nothing or not a lot in common with the approaches mentioned before. Often, they deal with social norms or accessibility in the form of e.g. facilitating conditions. Cheung, Chang et al. (2000) found support that facilitating conditions and social factors are two factors having a major influence on WWW usage. Facilitating conditions are considered to be relevant to the topic of personalised internet applications as well since they can be interpreted as the availability of necessary resources and support given by the system.

The Social-Economic-Psychological (SEP) model developed by Konana (included in Table 6) and the Balasubramanian (2005) model takes three perspectives, i.e. social, economic and psychological factors into consideration to explain trust, hedonic and utilitarian gains and in turn satisfaction. Although the model was intended to explain adoption and usage of technology for investors transacting online it can be of general significance by providing a multidisciplinary point of view on online consumer behaviour.

Table 6. Overview of Other HCI Approaches

Author/s and Publication Year	**Article title**	**Independent (Influencing) Variables**	**Dependent Variable (Outcome)**
Cheung, W. Chang, M.K. and V.S. Lai (2000)	Prediction of Internet and World Wide Web Usage at Work: A Test of an Extended Triandis Model	Facilitating Conditions, Social Factors, Affect, Consequences, Complexity	Current WWW Usage
Doll, W.J. and G. Torkzadeh (1988)	The Measurement of End-User Computing Satisfaction	Content, Accuracy, Format, Ease of Use, Timeliness	End-User Computing Satisfaction
Dos Santos, B.L. and M.L. Bariff (1988)	A Study of User Interface Aids for Model-Oriented DSS	Model Manipulation, Report Content, Presentation of Outcomes	Problem Identification and Prioritization
Hsu, M.-H. and C.-M. Chiu (2003)	Internet Self-Efficacy and Electronic Service Acceptance	Interpersonal Norm, Social Norm, Attitude, Web Self-Efficacy, Perceived Controllability	Intention => E-Service Usage
Liang, T.-P. and J.-S. Huang (1998)	An Empirical Study on Consumer Acceptance of Products in Electronic Markets: A Transaction Cost Model	Uncertainty, Asset Specifity, Transaction Cost	Acceptance (of Products in Electronic Markets)

Author/s and Publication Year	Article title	Independent (Influencing) Variables	Dependent Variable (Outcome)
Konana, P. and S. Balasubra-manian (2005)	The Social-Economic-Psychological Model of Technology Adoption and Usage: an Application to Online Investing	Social, Economic, Psychological Factors	Utilitarian Gains, Hedonic Gains, Trust => Satisfaction
Stone, R.W. and J.W. Henry (2003)	The Roles of Computer Self-Efficacy and Outcome Expectancy in Influencing the Computer End-User's Organizational Commitment	Computer Self-Efficacy, Outcome Expectancy	Organizational Commitment

An overview of different concepts applied to explain HCI and behaviour in computer-mediated environments (CMEs) was given. These approaches were helpful to develop the research model of this study. However, the author believes that none of these models can be used one-to-one to explain adoption, satisfaction or acceptance with personalised internet applications. Emerging factors such as trust or exploratory browsing behaviour have to be particularly considered. The next sub-chapter about design aspects is intended to give additional insights about possible evaluation factors and the assessment procedure.

2.5 User Interface Design Aspects

Effective web site design is an often employed term used in connection with web site satisfaction. The question arising is how does a web site design become efficient and satisfactory for the user? Several approaches are discussed and again, multi-disciplinary contributions can be found. Technical and functional requirements can play a crucial role. Obviously, user requirements are equally important and human-centred design (HCD) or user-centred design (UCD) approaches are applied more and more. Often the terms are used interchangeably but there are contributions highlighting a difference, e.g. in the way the technology is designed (Gasson, 2003). However, a quite common understanding of the Information Systems (IS) community is that the success of a system is proportional to the degree of user involvement in a system's design and development phase (Carmel, Whitaker, & George, 1993). Since this study focuses on user evaluation, only the user perspective of interface design will be discussed.

According to ISO 13407 (Kirakowski, 2003) human-centred design involves four key principles:

- The active involvement of users and specification of their requirements
- An appropriate allocation of function between users and technology
- Iterative design solutions (by receiving user feedback)
- Multi-disciplinary design (involving not only developers but also end-users and usability specialists).

For better illustration some examples of different design methods will be given. Participatory design (PD) is an approach originally developed for workplace information systems. There is no exact definition of PD; flexible practices are applied to include the user in the design process (Carmel et al., 1993). Contextual design or inquiry is a field study method researching the tasks and needs of users in their environment by e.g. observing them performing tasks (Smart & Whiting, 2001). Joint Application Design (JAD), a very popular design method involving user participation, employs several users to state their point of view in an organised manner of workshops or group meetings (Carmel et al., 1993; Davidson, 1999; Purvis & Sambamurthy, 1997).

Norman (2004) outlined in his book about Emotional Design three levels of design. First and most important, he mentioned visceral design meaning the physical features like how the web site looks and sounds. Second, he argued that behavioural design should be considered. This type of design is about using the web site and its performance. Behavioural design has basically four components: functions, understandability, usability and physical feeling. The last level, reflective design is about the meaning of a product service, the interaction and the long-term customer experience.

When speaking of design aspects often the term "usability" arises. Therefore, this topic will be outlined briefly. According to Lindgaard (1994) usability is defined as the ease of learning and using computer systems (for novices as well as for experienced users). In ISO (International Standards Organisation) 9241 (ISO, 1998) usability is "the extent to which a product can be used by specified users to achieve specified goals with effectiveness, efficiency and satisfaction in a specified context of use". In the author's opinion the definition "usability" is often used similarly with the construct perceived ease of use of the TAM. However, the definition of ISO is a broader one, covering more aspects than perceived ease of use. Usability becomes particularly important when focusing on the next chapter of system evaluation.

2.6 System Evaluation

This chapter is structured chronologically starting with software evaluation methods already developed before web site evaluation became an issue. The reason for the review is that useful methods or standard questionnaires could be borrowed for web site evaluation as well. The next sub-section is devoted to the specific topic of web site assessment.

2.6.1 Software Evaluation Methods

System and software evaluation became significant long ago before the Web discussion began with the goal to avoid user dissatisfaction or to increase employees' efficiency. According to ISO 9126 (ISO/IEC, 1991) there are six software quality characteristics: functionality, reliability, usability, efficiency, maintainability and portability. The factor which turned out to be most important (and which is often used as an overall term for all six characteristics named above) is definitely usability already mentioned in chapter 2.5 (Henderson, Podd, Smith, & Varela-Alvarez, 1995; Lin, Choong, & Salvendy, 1997). Usability is discussed and measured by numerous contributions (e.g. Lindgaard, 1994; Henderson et al., 1995; Oppermann and Reiterer, 1997; Lin et al., 1997).

Different categorisation approaches for software evaluation methods exists. A possibility is to distinguish between formative and summative evaluation. The first is the assessment of a system still in the prototype design stage whereas the latter focuses on a final, already fully operational system with the goal to measure efficacy or to compare two systems (Hartson, Andre, & Williges, 2001). Hilbert and Redmiles (2000) classified evaluation methods either if they are predictive, observational or participative. The first one includes cognitive walkthroughs or expert reviews. Observational evaluation is based on observation of users while testing a prototype or an already functioning system. The latter, participative evaluation is the collection of users' subjective opinions by questionnaires or interviews.

An adapted version of Oppermann and Reiterer's (1997) classification scheme for software evaluation will serve as a basis to distinguish between the broad categories of evaluation (see Table 7). Not all of the methods named in each category will be discussed in greater detail; the attention will be paid to the most popular methods.

Table 7. Classification of Software Evaluation Methods (Oppermann & Reiterer, 1997)

Subjective evaluation methods
❖ Questionnaires
❖ Interviews
Objective evaluation methods
❖ Observations
❖ Video recording
❖ Interaction based (e.g. logging)
Expert evaluation methods
❖ Checklists and guidelines
❖ (Cognitive) walkthroughs
❖ Specialists reports and heuristic evaluation
Experimental evaluation methods

Starting with subjective evaluation methods, questionnaires are popular and widespread to collect user opinions. Usability plays a central role when evaluating a system. According to Dillon (2003), the term "Usability Testing" in a general sense means all kind of User Interface (UI) inspection methods such as heuristic evaluations, expert reviews and cognitive walkthroughs. Usability testing in a more specific sense describes an evaluation procedure, which comprises the performing of tasks by users. Several contributions exist which contain some kind of "standard questionnaires" facilitating the evaluation of a system. They were created to have a reliable tool measuring the users' point of view and covering all relevant areas of system evaluation. Approaches range from very simple and quick questionnaires, e.g. the System Usability Scale (SUS, Brooke, 1986), Nielsen's Heuristic Evaluation and Nielsen's Attributes of Usability (Nielsen, 1993) - to more comprehensive ones. The Software Usability Measurement Inventory (SUMI, Human Factors Research Group, 2002) contains around 50 questions, the Questionnaire for User Interaction Satisfaction (QUIS, Chin et al., 1988) covers five areas to be rated: overall reactions to the system, screen, terminology and system information, learning and system capabilities. IBM developed some usability satisfaction questionnaires (Lewis, 1995): the After-Scenario Questionnaire (ASQ), the Post-Study System Usability Questionnaire (PSSUQ) and the Computer System Usability Questionnaire (CSUQ). The Purdue Usability Testing Questionnaire (PUTQ) was designed to evaluate the usability of all kind of software products (Lin et al., 1997). The questionnaire is very extensive using 100 questions to gain knowledge about a system's consistency, flexibility, learnability or user guidance. Table 8 gives an overview of the topics covered by PUTQ and a few example questions for each area.

The second subjective assessment approach, the interview, is often time-, cost and/or staff-intensive although it can be productive by giving new insights (which would not be covered by a pre-defined questionnaire) because the interviewer can ask specific issues of concern (Shneiderman, 1992). Interviews are particularly useful when the study is an exploratory one (Oppermann and Reiterer, 1997).

Objective evaluation methods include observations which can be either realised in the field or in the laboratory. Since observations are complex tasks, they are often complemented by video-taping or the logging of data (Lindgaard, 1994). Video-taping is a useful method because every reaction of the user such as eye-movements can be tracked and analyzed. The use of an automated data tracking method by collecting and analysing usage data seems to be the most comprehensive approach of objective evaluation methods. All possible interactions can be tracked: e.g. number of errors, trials, task time.

Expert evaluation methods range from simple guideline or checklist reviews to more extensive approaches. The cognitive walkthrough is a technique for evaluating the design of a user interface, with special attention to how well the interface supports "exploratory learning," i.e., first-time use without formal training (Rieman, Franzke, & Redmiles, 1995). According to Ivory and Hearst (2001) the expert has to simulate users' problem solving. In the cognitive walkthrough, the sequence of actions refers to the steps that an interface will require a user to go through in order to accomplish some task. The evaluators then step through that action sequence to check for potential usability problems.

Table 8. An overview of PUTQ areas with example questions (Lin et al., 1997)

Compatibility Is the wording familiar? Is the control matched to user skill?
Consistency Is the feedback consistent? Is the wording consistent with user guidance?
Flexibility Does it provide flexible user guidance? Are users allowed to customize windows?
Learnability Is the ordering of menu options logical? Is the data grouping reasonable for easy learning?
Minimal Action Does it provide default values? Does it require minimal steps in sequential menu selection?
Minimal Memory Load Are selected data highlighted? Are prior answers recapitulated?
Perceptual Limitation Does it provide easily distinguished colours? Are groups of information demarcated?
User Guidance Is HELP provided? System feedback: how helpful is the error message?

Another technique, the heuristic evaluation, is defined by Lindgaard (1994) as a detailed informal subjective usability analysis conducted by experts simulating the perspective of a typical end user. The evaluators do not follow a specific set of methods, rules or procedures; instead they rely on a set of vague guidelines. By performing a heuristic evaluation the experts identify violations of certain heuristics, i.e. some pre-defined principles (Ivory and Hearst, 2001). In addition to the cognitive walkthrough, the heuristic evaluation is an in-depth analysis collecting all occurred problems, from the highly serious to the most trivial. However, the judgements of experts underlie some subjectivity and are influenced by their experience, background and talent in anticipating what a user finds easy or difficult when using a system (Oppermann and Reiterer, 1997).

Lindgaard (1994) distinguishes various data collection methods for usability testing being classified by the time of collection and if the data collection is conducted in the field or laboratory (see Figure 10).

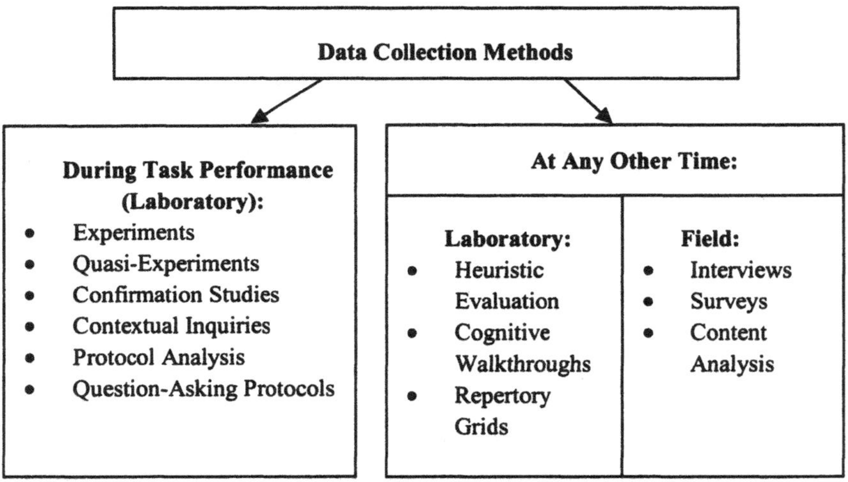

Figure 10. Examples of Data Collection Methods for Usability Testing (adapted from Lindgaard 1994)

Experiments can be classified as a method in which the experimental situation is exactly defined; a main characteristic is the variation of the independent variables. However, with quasi-experiments the experimenter does not exert control over all of the variables (Lindgaard, 1994). Confirmation studies serve as an assessment of usability defects detected in heuristic evaluations. The goal when performing contextual inquiries is to discover design opportunities during user interactions. A protocol analysis is a record of test person's comments, suggestions, or problems occurred with a system. When question-asking protocols are employed to assess usability; predetermined questions are asked (Lindgaard, 1994).

The laboratory data collection methods heuristic evaluation and cognitive walkthrough were already described above. Applying the technique of repertory grids means that different systems or tasks are proposed and test persons make judgements about differences or similarities. As far as the field methods are concerned the often applied techniques, interview and survey, have to be mentioned.

This sub-section was intended to give an overview about software and usability evaluation methods. The next sub-section focuses more specifically on the assessment of web sites and possible techniques.

2.6.2 Web Site Evaluation Methods

The knowledge about a web site's effectiveness is essential to make improvements and to have a successful site. Therefore, the need for an appropriate evaluation method is obvious. An assessment is simply a necessity, a prerequisite to discover strengths and weaknesses. A number of studies on the effectiveness of web sites were already conducted. They range from simple rankings, awards, guidelines to highly complex evaluations. An overview of different web site evaluation methods will be given.

A possible distinguishing factor is whether qualitative measures such as protocol analysis (e.g. Benbunan-Fich, 2001) or quantitative methods like web site metrics (e.g. Olsina and Rossi, 2001, Ivory et al., 2000, Wöber et al., 2002) are applied. Although qualitative investigations allow gaining deeper insights of specific problems occurring; they tend to be more subjective and less comparable. Quantitative Web site evaluation can be performed in the way of judging site structure, technical parameters, and content or server characteristics. Predetermined categories and attributes are used to assess the Web. Log file analysis is a typical example of a method relying solely on a quantitative data collection by using traffic-based characteristics to establish usage patterns. Applying these quantitative evaluation methods the evaluation process is likely to be structured, accurate and comprehensible (Olsina and Rossi, 2001).

A lot of efforts have been made in developing quantitative approaches for web site measurement. These contributions range from developing bench-marking metrics or specifications (e.g. Ivory et al., 2001, Johnson and Misic, 1999, Jutla et al., 1999) to highly sophisticated Web mining tools. They can provide useful preliminary work (data) to web site evaluations by extracting different information from web sites.

A large research area consisting of automated quantitative web site analysis was developed by means of Web mining methods. Originally, Web mining methods stem from the large research field of data mining. Data mining is defined as the extraction and the discovery of previously unknown but useful and interesting information and interrelations in large databases as to infer new knowledge (Nestorov & Tsur, 1999; Spiliopoulou, 2000). Web mining enables the systematic discovery, extraction and analysis of WWW information sources (Cooley, Mobasher, & Srivastava, 1997; Kosala & Blockeel, 2000). Figure 11 illustrates that Web mining consists of three areas (Srivastava, Cooley, Deshpande, & Tan, 2000; Zaiane, 1998).

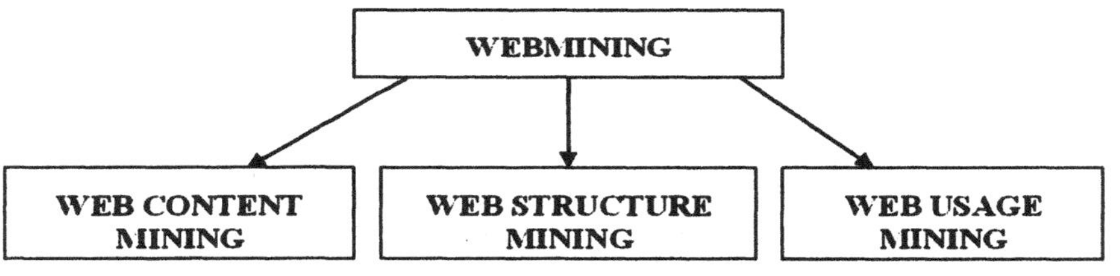

Figure 11. Three Areas of Webmining

Web content mining is defined as the discovery and analysis of content and data of the Web. Web structure mining is concerned with the structure of hyperlinks, whereas the latter, web usage mining analyses the user behaviour (Kosala and Blockeel, 2000).

A qualitative method which can be found quite often is the think aloud method or protocol analysis (e.g. Benbunan-Fich, 2001; Van Waes, 2001). Test persons are asked to say what they are thinking about the Web site they are surfing or if problems are occurring. Although protocol analysis is a feasible and efficient approach (Benbunan-Fich, 2001) there are also some drawbacks like that the situation can be quite unnatural for the test persons. A variation of the think-aloud verbal protocol analysis is the co-operative evaluation technique. Users and designers assess a system together; users are encouraged to ask questions during the interaction with the system. Similarly, evaluators can ask the user questions if problems or misunderstandings are occurring or at any other time during the evaluation (Marsh & Wright, 1999; Yong & Kong, 1999). The obvious advantage is that the process is more natural than the 'pure' think-aloud method. Additionally, more insights can be gained because the evaluator can immediately ask about problems when he or she recognises any dissatisfaction of the user. Another popular qualitative method of web site evaluation is the cognitive walkthrough (e.g. discussed in Blackmon et al., 2002 or applied in Jacobsen and John, 2000) as already outlined before.

A further difference already mentioned above is if the assessment was conducted by automated tools or if a manual method (e.g. expert review) was chosen. While manual methods for system assessment can be valuable giving deeper insight, this type of evaluation is time-consuming and complex (particularly if a large number of web sites are to be evaluated). Besides, a certain degree of subjectivity cannot be completely avoided. An automated data gathering process is an invaluable opportunity for assessing dynamic media such as the World Wide Web (Scharl, 2000).

Olsina (2003) divided evaluation methods by categories, i.e.: testing, inspection, inquiry and simulation. A similar categorisation can be found in Ivory (2003). The respective methods for each category (derived from Ivory, 2003, Nielsen, 1993, Olsina, 2003) are shown in Table 9.

As far as the data collection used for this study is concerned the method of inquiry, a user survey, will be applied. First, study participants are asked to do a pre-determined task simulating real problem solving with a personalised internet application. Afterwards they are asked to evaluate the system according to usability and HCI issues by answering a questionnaire. The questionnaire finishes with some general demographic and internet usage questions. The procedure will be further outlined in Chapter 4.

Table 9. Web Site Evaluation Methods by Categories (Ivory, 2003, Nielsen, 1993, Olsina, 2003)

- **Testing**
  - *Thinking-Aloud-Protocol* (Users talk aloud while testing a Web site)
  - *Testing of System Performance* (e.g. speed)
  - *Web Log-File Analysis* (data recording of a user interaction)
  - *Remote Testing* (users and evaluators are separated)
  - *Contents Testing* (relevancy, consistency, timeliness of the content)

• **Inspection** (performed by one or more experts) – *Guideline Review* – *Heuristic Evaluation* (review of usability principles, i.e. heuristics) and *Estimation* (an evaluators' prediction of usability) – *Cognitive Walkthrough* (simulation of users' problem solving task) – *Feature, Consistency, Standards and Formal Usability Inspection* (e.g. review of ISO standards)
• **Inquiry** – *Field Observation* (users interact with a site in their environment) – *Questionnaires* (standard questionnaires such as PSSUQ, SUMI) – *User Feedback* (users submit comments and suggestions) – *Focus Groups* (user discussion)
• **Simulation Methods** (Simulation of a user-site interaction)

3 INFLUENCES ON PERSONALISED INTERNET APPLICATIONS' SATISFACTION - RESEARCH MODEL AND HYPOTHESES

This chapter deals with the conceptual model of the study and the hypotheses which form the basis of the analysis. A definition for each of the employed dimensions is given and the reasons why the particular influencing factors were chosen are discussed. Furthermore, the items employed to measure the respective dimensions are outlined.

3.1 Research Model

The research question of this study stems from the gap that the previously named models about HCI, e.g. the TAM is often investigated in an isolated way. At best, they are extended by some factors, e.g. web security and access costs (Shih, 2004) or perceived enjoyment (Teo et al., 1999). These models are well researched, valuable, and provide a substantial contribution to the explanation of system usage and/or satisfaction. However, they do not acknowledge the full variety of influences for the particular case of personalised internet applications. Thus, the major goal of this paper is to test a merged model including factors of the TAM and additionally adding two personal influencing factors: attitude and experience. However, the model does not yet cover any hedonic needs and fun factors or security concerns. Thus, the model was enhanced to explain more influencing factors. The concept of trust is added since its influence on personalised internet applications and e-commerce sites (on which products and services can be purchased) is crucial. Finally, the model is extended by exploratory behaviour covering the hedonic aspects of a web site visit. Figure 12 gives an overview of the main components included in the extended model.

Another objective of this study is to develop a model explaining user satisfaction with personalised internet applications. Many attempts were undertaken to evaluate websites but only a few concentrate on more intelligent systems like personalised internet applications. However, these kinds of systems require a particular careful and thorough assessment since they are intended to perform personalised services like recommendations. Furthermore, there are features of special relevance to personalised systems. The experiential aspect plays a much greater role than for ordinary web sites because personalised applications are often employed to fulfil not only goal-directed purposes but enable inspiration as well. Finally, it is hypothesised that trust towards the web site (and information processing) has a higher significance because personal data are revealed.

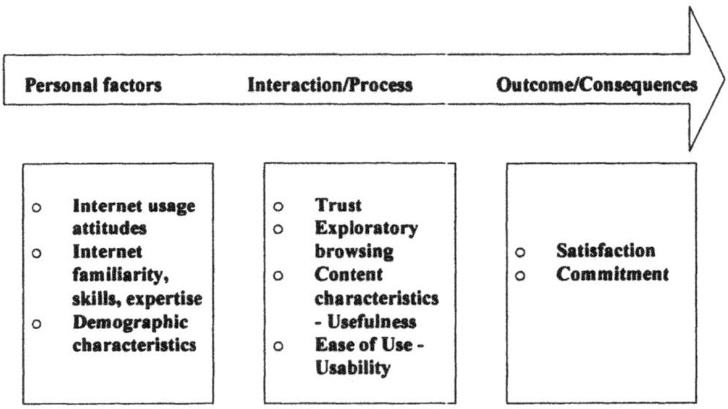

Figure 12. Components of the Conceptual Model

Figure 12 depicts the model components of this study. The influencing factors are divided into personal factors denoting the characteristics of the individual which cannot be influenced by the internet application provider. Second, there are the interaction/process characteristics which could be optimised by the web site provider. Finally, both of these characteristics do have an influence on the outcome, i.e. satisfaction with the personalised internet application and the commitment to use it again or to recommend it.

Furthermore, the relationships of these factors are of obvious importance. Which of the factors outlined above influence each other either directly or indirectly? In Figure 13 the research model and its hypothesised relationships are presented. Two competing constructs are exploratory browsing behaviour and enjoyment. Since exploratory browsing behaviour is hypothesised to be the more appropriate construct in the context of personalised internet applications, enjoyment is shown only by dotted lines in the research model. A research model including perceived enjoyment with the personalised internet applications will serve as an alternative model.

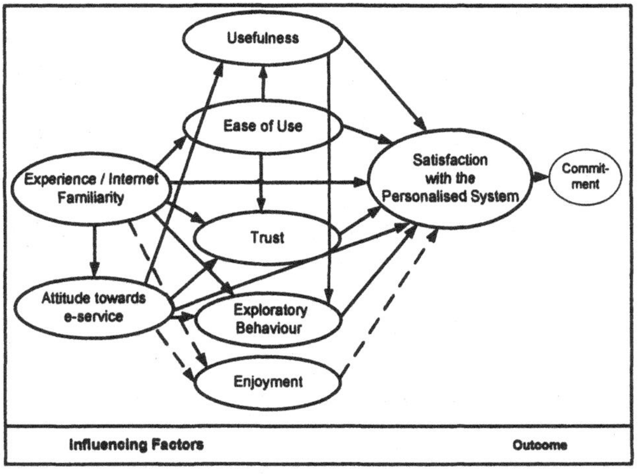

Figure 13. The Research Model

Literature review suggested that the constructs investigated in this study have an impact on satisfaction. All of the constructs are explained and the operationalisations used for each dimension are presented in the following section.

3.2 Influencing Factors – Constructs and Hypotheses

Each construct will be outlined and the reasons why it is included in the model are presented. Of course, there are several indirect relationships and some of the influencing factors do have an impact on each other (as can be seen in Figure 13). Furthermore, hypotheses about the structure of the model are outlined. Starting with usefulness and ease of use (or information quality and system quality), these are clearly one of the most important and most researched influencing factors for system usage and satisfaction.

3.2.1 Perceived Usefulness

Perceived usefulness (PU) was defined by Davis (1989) as the user's assessment that applying a particular system will increase his or her job performance. The original study of Davis was conducted in a work-related environment. However, the construct of perceived usefulness was tested with software, information systems (e.g. Bhattacherjee and Premkumar 2004), or web sites as well (e.g. Morosan and Jeong, 2006, Teo, et al., 1999 and many more). DeLone and McLean (1992) tested a similar construct they called information quality. They defined information quality as the IS output, the quality of the information. However, the construct name used in this study will be usefulness because it is better known and the author believes that usefulness is a more meaningful term than information quality. The definition employed is that using a particular personalised internet application will help to solve a specific task satisfactorily and that accurate, meaningful and helpful information is provided. The hypothesis is that the more useful a user perceives a system the higher the satisfaction will be (H1a).

The dimension of usefulness covers the following measurement items (the German version of the items are found in the appendix, a summary of all of the dimensions, their items and references are found in chapter 4.2 Development of the survey instrument):

- ❖ Overall, I find this web site being useful.
- ❖ The use of Learn@WU / immobilien.net / Tiscover did facilitate my search for learning materials / real estate / a travel.
- ❖ This web site enables me to quickly find interesting information.
- ❖ This web site is increasing the quality of my information search.

Chung and Tan (2004) found out in their study about the antecedents of playfulness that content plays a major role when thinking of playfulness. In this study, exploratory browsing behaviour is considered instead of playfulness. Nevertheless, it is expected that usefulness serves as an antecedent for exploratory browsing behaviour as well constituting hypothesis 1b. The rationale behind this hypothesis is the suggestion that only if a personalised internet application is perceived to be useful exploratory browsing is induced.

H1a Perceived Usefulness is hypothesised to have a positive direct influence on satisfaction with a personalised internet application (PIA).

H1b Perceived Usefulness is hypothesised to have a positive direct influence on exploratory browsing behaviour.

3.2.2 Perceived Ease of Use

Perceived ease of use (PEOU) refers to the user's impression that using a particular system would be free of effort (Davis, 1989). DeLone and McLean (1992) define their construct "system quality as the quality characteristics of the system itself". The concept of usability is similar to the constructs of system quality and PEOU. However, often it refers to more issues than PEOU, e.g. the norm ISO 9241 (ISO, 1998) defines usability as using a system with effectiveness, efficiency and satisfaction. The construct chosen in this study is perceived ease of use referring to the narrower concept. The definition of ease of use is that the system's use is possible without great effort and the system's use is easy to learn, e.g. the navigation path is clear. The influence of PEOU on Usefulness (H2c) was confirmed in a lot of studies (e.g. Davis, 1989, Legris, et al., 2003). Furthermore, Koufaris and Hampton-Sosa (2004) showed in their study that PEOU constitutes a weak but significant influence on trust which is therefore, proposed as hypothesis H2b in this study. Finally, it is hypothesised that PEOU exerts a direct positive influence on satisfaction with a PIA (H2a).

H2a Perceived Ease of Use positively influences the satisfaction with a personalised internet application.

H2b Perceived Ease of Use positively influences the level of trust with a personalised internet application.

H2c Perceived Usefulness is influenced positively by Perceived Ease of Use.

EOU is measured in this study by the following items:

- Overall, I find this web site easy to use.
- This web site is user friendly.
- It is easy to learn how to use this web site.
- The structure of the web site is confusing.

3.2.3 Trust

Privacy and security concerns play an increasing role. Does the user trust the web site provider, the information and the way how transactions are done? Is there anything which could jeopardise trust in a web site such as logging and tracking of personal data and misusing them afterwards? How is the trustworthiness of information, of recommendations, the careful treatment of sensitive data, credit card transactions assessed by the users?

A lot of fraud incidents and attacks annoy users. A widely known example is e-mail spam. Unfortunately phishing attacks (i.e. an e-mail looking officially which is intended to convince the user to reveal passwords, PINs at a manipulated website (http://www.webopedia.com, online encyclopaedia)) or identity theft practices became well known recently. Bogus web sites (web sites offering products or services which do not exist or which disseminate misinformation), fake websites (being copies of web sites, they look the same or use similar URIs but have different contents) are other examples of the misuse of the Internet.

Trust was investigated and proven to be important by a lot of studies (e.g. Chiou, 2004, Pavlou, 2001, Yoon, 2002, Kimery and McCord, 2002) and its significance will even rise because more and more people use the Internet for financial transactions. Urban et al. (2000) argued that among others trust building cues should be used. The provision of complete and unbiased information is crucial. Furthermore, virtual-advisor technologies can increase customers' trust in the web site. The authors are even convinced that trust presents the key to online success. Hoffman et al. (1999) concluded that trust is an important issue with 95% of users have already refused to reveal personal information at web sites. Whereas 58% of Americans have trust in newspaper and television the amount of trust is dramatically decreasing when thinking of the Internet: only 26% trust online commerce sites (Carton, 2002). Even when a low risk purchase e.g. a book is bought online, trust is a significant influencing factor (Gefen, 2000). Examples from the Internet banking area show that trust does have a tremendous impact on the attitude towards using a banking service in an online environment (Suh & Han, 2002). Pavlou and Chai (2002) found out that trust has a significant influence on attitude and perceived behavioural control although it varies across cultures.

Therefore, the websites do not only need to have high security standards but also need to give the impression that one can trust that the information is processed securely. However, there is another aspect of trustworthiness: trust is required concerning the information on the web site and the recommendations given by the system. If a user does not trust in the recommendations, it is not very likely that she/he will buy the goods/services proposed.

Trust is the subjective assessment of a user that the website provider will perform a transaction in accordance with the user's confident expectations (Ba & Pavlou, 2002). Gefen (2000) argued that trust towards an online provider is making oneself vulnerable to actions of the provider based on confidence and assurance.

Trust is defined in this study as the users believe that his or her inquiry will be treated according to his confident expectations concerning security issues.

The concept of trust proposed in this study covers the following aspects:

- Trust towards the information indicated on the web site
- Trust concerning the provision of personal information
- Trust towards the security of the system
- How are the security standards of the web site?
- Trust towards the recommendations / proposals given

H3 Trust positively influences the satisfaction with a personalised internet application.

3.2.4 Exploratory Browsing Behaviour

Hedonic components of the web site experience are represented in this study by exploratory browsing behaviour. While various models in the HCI field try to capture the hedonic side of the on-line experiences by integrating variables such as fun, entertainment, playfulness, pleasure, or emotions in general, they do not fully acknowledge the advances in explaining consumer and especially information behaviour already elaborated. Furthermore, as personalised systems being a special form of a web site, they should encourage variety-seeking behaviour and users' browsing. Even in an e-learning context, exploratory browsing or enjoyment play a role not to be neglected (Lee, Cheung, & Chen, 2005).

Inspired by Baumgartner and Steenkamp (1996), Steenkamp et al. (2002), Steenkamp and Burgess (1996) and Huang (2000) the definition of exploratory browsing behaviour used in this study is: EBB is understood as being an inducement for the user to browse the web site because inspiration is offered, variety or novelty-seeking desires are satisfied or excitement is created.

The construct EBB was measured by the following items:

- Variety-seeking: The visit of the web site offered me variety.
- Inspiration: This web site inspired me.
- Curiosity: This web site induced curiosity.
- Excitement: The use of the web site was exciting.
- Novelty-seeking: The web site offered novel information / products to me.
- Pleasure: Using the web site was a pleasure.

H4 Exploratory Browsing Behaviour positively influences the satisfaction with a personalised internet application.

Furthermore, enjoyment will serve as a competing construct to exploratory browsing behaviour.

3.2.5 Enjoyment

When compared to exploratory browsing behaviour, enjoyment is certainly the construct more often used in the Web context (e.g. Van der Heijden 2004, Yi and Hwang, 2003). However, it is hypothesised that exploratory browsing behaviour in the WWW context is another appropriate construct suggested by a previous study (Bauernfeind & Zins, 2006). Since EBB is not as well tested as enjoyment, enjoyment will be used as well to assure that the hedonic component of web site satisfaction is not neglected in this study. Furthermore, these two dimensions will be tested as competing ones. The definition of enjoyment used in this study was inspired by van der Heijden (2004) and Davis, et al. (1992). According to them enjoyment is driven by intrinsic motivations and is the degree to which a system's use is personally enjoyable and fun.

Enjoyment is measured by the following items:

- This web site induces new ideas.
- This web site enhances my creativity.
- This web site arouses my imagination.

H4a Enjoyment positively influences the satisfaction with a personalised internet application.

Finally, the personal characteristics, attitude towards e-service and experience with the Internet are included in the research model. They are hypothesised to influence satisfaction and commitment either directly or indirectly.

3.2.6 Attitude towards e-service

Attitude was considered in a number of studies to serve as an influencing factor on satisfaction, performance or behavioural intention to use (e. g. Eroglu, et al., 2003, Shih, 2004, Suh and Han, 2002). Attitude can be the general attitude towards using the Internet or more specific towards information search on the web. Furthermore, the attitude towards the usage of the Internet to perform specific tasks (e.g. searching for a travel, buying a book) or the attitude towards e-shopping could be involved as well. In this study the attitude towards the usage of e-services is investigated. Attitude towards the usage of e-services is defined as the positive or negative attitude towards information acquiring via the WWW in general and for a specific product / service. Furthermore, the process of problem solving is covered as well meaning what is the user's attitude towards the e-service concerning a specific task.

The items used to measure the construct of attitude towards the e-service are:

- Information acquisition through the web is too time-consuming.
- Information acquisition via the web is useful.
- Using the web to solve this specific problem/task was a good idea.

The personal characteristic attitude towards the usage of e-services is hypothesised to have on the one hand a direct influence on satisfaction with the personalised system. On the other hand, attitude will influence how other constructs, i.e. ease of use, trust, usefulness and exploratory browsing are perceived.

H5a Attitude influences the satisfaction with a personalised internet application.

H5b Attitude has an influence on the level of trust.

H5c Attitude will influence exploratory browsing behaviour.

H5d The more positive the attitude towards e-services or online information search is the more useful a personalised internet application will be perceived.

3.2.7 Experience

Experience with a system software, the web in general or a specific web site was considered in a number of studies (e.g. Igbaria and Iivari, 1995, Rodgers, et al., 2005, Wöber, et al., 2002, Gefen, 2000, Gefen and Straub, 2004). The Internet experience or familiarity in general could be considered or the familiarity (previous experience) with a particular interface could be the focus. In this study the internet familiarity in general is covered and additionally the familiarity with the particular personalised internet application is measured.

The questions used for the construct of experience / internet familiarity were:

- I feel familiar with the web site because of previous usage.
- How often do you use the WWW on average?
- Do you consider yourself as an experienced user of the WWW?

Again, experience can either serve as a direct influencer on the outcome or as an antecedent of other constructs or both, e.g. the influence of experience on trust was investigated by Riegelsberger et al. (2005). Wöber, et al. (2002) suggested that perceived ease of use and usefulness are influenced by experience. Furthermore, it is suggested that the level of experience exerts an influence on the attitude towards e-service or online information search. The higher the experience level the more favourable will be the attitude. All of the following hypotheses are suggested to be positive.

H6a Experience influences the satisfaction with a personalised internet application.

H6b Experience influences the perception of ease of use.

H6c Experience has an influence on the level of trust.

H6d Experience will influence exploratory browsing behaviour.

H6e Experience will influence the attitude towards online information search and e-service.

Other personal characteristics than attitude and experience could be considered. Accessibility and facilitating conditions do not only mean physical access to the medium Internet. Access costs are a factor not to be neglected but there are also other aspects covered by accessibility, e.g. the possibility for disabled people to use a website. The importance of accessibility in the way of physical access or technical barriers is diminishing more and more in Western Europe. Bandwidths are improving continuously and more people gain access to the internet.

Involvement is another personal characteristic which could be considered when evaluating user satisfaction, systems' success or purchase intention via the Internet (e.g. Goldsmith, 2002, Hwang and Thorn, 1999, Palanisamy and Sushil, 2001, Blili et al., 1998, Lin and Shao, 2000). Involvement can be described twofold: first, the situational involvement when using the site, when interacting and searching for a particular service or product. Second, it means also product involvement, the general interest for a product or service. However, in this study, it is proposed to create a certain level of situational involvement by asking the study participants to perform a specific task on the personalised internet application.

3.2.8 Satisfaction

Finally, the two outcome criteria satisfaction and commitment are outlined. Satisfaction was defined by Oliver and Shankar et al. (1999; 2003) as "the perception of pleasurable fulfilment of a service". Satisfaction covers in this study the overall contentment with the personalised internet application after the user has experienced it.

The measures used for satisfaction were:

- the overall impression of the web site
- success of the information search process
- positive overall experience with the web site
- the quality of the recommendations / proposals was convincing
- the web site meets expectations

E-satisfaction was often researched in connection to e-loyalty, e.g. (Anderson & Srinivasan, 2003; Shankar et al., 2003). Loyalty is defined as a deep commitment to the provider (Oliver, 1999; Shankar et al., 2003). This study focuses not only on the aspect of intention to revisit the site but also on further recommendation to others. Therefore, the concept proposed is called commitment which is outlined in the next section.

The hypothesis emanating from satisfaction is that it has a positive influence on commitment.

H7 Satisfaction will positively influence commitment, with greater satisfaction leading to higher commitment.

3.2.9 Commitment

Commitment focuses on two aspects: the intention of the user to revisit the internet application and the willingness to recommend the web site to others (relatives, friends, colleagues).

The following items were used to measure this construct:

- I can recommend this web site.
- I will revisit this web site.
- I will use this web site more often in the future.

Literature review suggested the supposed relationships and influencing factors. Applied to the context of personalised internet applications, they are hypothetical. The goal of this study is to investigate these influences and to develop a valid model covering factors influencing satisfaction with personalised internet applications. The following chapter will outline the study methodology.

4 STUDY METHODOLOGY

This chapter gives an overview of the research methods, the development of the survey instrument and the personalised internet applications used for the evaluation. Furthermore, the procedure of the user evaluations is outlined. How were the study participants recruited and which were the data collection methods?

The study focuses on the influencing factors for satisfaction with personalised internet applications. Thus, three PIAs were used to test satisfaction of test persons and the hypothesised relationships. Based on the findings of this analysis, expert opinions were collected to obtain an additional point of view on the importance of the factors investigated and future possible developments.

4.1 Research Methods

4.1.1 Qualitative versus quantitative research methods

The first question arising is if for the intended study either a qualitative or a quantitative approach is more appropriate to solve the research question. The distinction between qualitative and quantitative approach which arises first, is that quantitative research methods use countable data. The aim is to collect data about quantifiable dimensions whereas qualitative techniques use "rich" information meaning words or pictures (Middleton, 1995). Thus, the gathering of data is different: quantitative data collection is limited to predetermined categories, obtains data for example through standard questionnaires whereas qualitative ones are not constrained to predetermined categories and use methods such as in depth-interviews (Neumann, 1997). What are the implications, advantages, shortcomings and the resulting areas of application of these statements? One of the most significant distinctions is that quantitative approaches permit statistical analysis but qualitative methodologies are less or not appropriate to collect quantifiable results (Myers, 2005). Thus, results of quantitative research are easier to compare and more precise whereas qualitative methods generally allow deeper insight in the subject to be investigated; for example it is possible to explore attitudes, feelings, perceptions (Skinner, Tagg, & Holloway, 2000). Quantitative methods are principally used to obtain information about a large number of objects to be investigated whereas qualitative ones seem more appropriate for a collection of "rich" information about a smaller amount of objects to be investigated. Qualitative techniques are less useful if the aim of obtaining statements or generalisations about a relatively large population is pursued (Veal, 1994). However, both approaches are valuable and can complement each other.

4.1.2 Approaches Used in this Study

Both approaches are used in this study. A quantitative approach was applied to obtain a large number of user data to test the hypotheses named in the previous chapter. A web-based survey was used to collect user opinions about the personalised internet applications after the test persons had completed a pre-determined task.

Furthermore, qualitative expert opinions were collected to get a broader picture what might be important in the future and what are the challenges and opportunities for providers of PIA. Based on the results of the quantitative analysis of the user data, the experts were asked to give their opinions about current and future importance of each of the constructs as well as their perceptions of further important issues concerning personalised internet applications. The method of in-depth interviews was used. The qualitative research technique of the in-depth interviews allows getting deeper insights into experts' point of views, thoughts and perspectives (Guion, 2006).

4.2 Development of the Survey Instrument

First, a literature review was done to discover items which could be useful for the quantitative part of the study. For each of the research model's constructs about 15 items were chosen, translated and pre-tested. Two pre-tests were conducted to assure the proper realisation of the main survey. The goal of the first pre-test was to test which items are appropriate for the respective constructs. Approximately 150 students tested these items. After doing the first pre-test, the questions most appropriate were chosen. 4 to 6 items which loaded best were used to operationalise the constructs in the main survey. Furthermore, the web site providers were asked if they have additional questions they want to add and if yes, these were included as well. All the items of the main survey and the pre-tests were measured on a 4-point Likert scale (ranging from "I totally agree" to "I totally disagree"). As soon as the questionnaire was designed the second pre-test was conducted focusing on the procedure and comprehensibility of the survey, the questions and the task. 15 colleagues and friends were asked if the pre-determined task and the questions are clear and understandable. The questions and tasks were slightly changed according to the results of the second pre-test.

The following table shows the questions used in the final questionnaire. They were either taken one to one from the source or more often they were slightly changed to fit the context. The questions were translated and they were re-formulated to be applicable for the specific web site, e.g. instead of "Using the web excites my curiosity." (Shang et al., 2005) the question "This web site excited my curiosity." was used.

Some questions were created because no appropriate questions used in previous studies were found (indicated in Table 10 as "own source"). Instead of using the term "personalised internet application" in the questions the more general term "web site" was used. It was assumed that the majority of the study participants do not have the knowledge what makes a personalised internet application different from a web site. Therefore, it was refrained from using this term.

Table 10. Constructs and their Measurement Items

Dimen-sion	Operationalisation	Reference
Ease of Use	Overall, I find this web site easy to use.	(Davis, 1989)
	This web site is user friendly.	(Muylle, Moenaert, & Despontin, 2004; Stone & Henry, 2003)
	It is easy to learn how to use this web site.	(Davis, 1989; Lewis, 1995)
	The structure of the web site is confusing.	(Muylle et al., 2004)

Dimen -sion	Operationalisation	Reference
Usefulness	Overall, I find this web site being useful.	(Davis, 1989)
	The use of Learn@WU / immobilien.net / Tiscover did facilitate my search for learning materials / real estate / a travel.	(Hsu & Chiu, 2003)
	This web site enables me to quickly find interesting information.	(Davis, 1989)
	This web site is increasing the quality of my information search.	(Hsu & Chiu, 2003; Stone & Henry, 2003)
Exploratory Browsing Behaviour	The visit of the web site offered me variety.	(Novak et al., 2000)
	This web site inspired me.	(Agarwal & Karahanna, 2000; 2005)
	This web site excited my curiosity.	(Agarwal & Karahanna, 2000; Baumgartner & Steenkamp, 1996; Novak et al., 2000; Shang et al., 2005)
	The use of the web site was exciting to me.	(Teo et al., 1999)
	The web site offered novel information / products to me.	(Richard, 2005; Skadberg & Kimmel, 2004)
	Using the web site was a pleasure.	(Teo et al., 1999)
Enjoyment	This web site induces new ideas.	(own source)
	This web site enhances my creativity.	(Novak et al., 2000)

Dimen -sion	Operationalisation	Reference
	This web site arouses my imagination.	(Agarwal & Karahanna, 2000; Novak et al., 2000)
Trust	This web site conveys the feeling that personal information is treated confidentially.	(Kim & Stoel, 2004; Wang, Tang, & Tang, 2001; Yoon, 2002)
	I trust the information indicated on the web site.	(Pavlou & Fygenson, 2006; Stewart, 2003)
	I have the impression that the web site www.immobilien.net / https://learn.wu-wien.ac.at / www.tiscover.at is secure.	(Wang et al., 2001)
	The web site seems like being equipped with the best security standards.	(Koufaris & Hampton-Sosa, 2004)
	The proposals (searching results) of the web site were convincing.	(own source)
Attitude	Information acquisition through the web is too time-consuming.	(Cheung et al., 2000)
	Information acquisition via the web is useful.	(own source)
	I think it was a good idea to use the web for that type of task.	(Hsu & Chiu, 2003; Suh & Han, 2002)
Experience / Internet Familiarity	I feel familiar with the web site because of previous usage.	(Gefen & Straub, 2004)
	How often do you use the WWW on average?	(Cheung et al., 2000; Lederer et al., 2000; Teo et al., 1999)
	Do you consider yourself as an experienced user of the WWW?	(own source)

Dimen -sion	Operationalisation	Reference
Satisfaction	I am satisfied with the outcome of my information search.	(McKinney, Yoon, & Zahedi, 2002)
	Overall, I made some positive experiences with the use of Learn @WU / www.immobilien.net / www.tiscover.at.	(Bhattacherjee, 2001)
	The quality of the proposals / searching results was convincing.	(Bauernfeind & Zins, 2006)
	This web site meets my expectations.	(Anderson & Srinivasan, 2003; Lewis, 1995)
	Overall, how is your impression of this web site? (global satisfaction item)	(McKinney et al., 2002)
Commitment	I can recommend this web site.	(Suh & Han, 2002)
	I will revisit this web site.	(Pavlou, 2001; Suh & Han, 2002)
	I will use this web site more often in the future.	(Suh & Han, 2002)

4.3 Internet Applications Used for Evaluation

The evaluation was based on three personalised internet applications. Some background information will be provided for each of them. Furthermore, the reasons why these particular systems from that particular industry were chosen will be outlined.

The three personalised internet applications have in common that they offer assistance and guidance to the user through a variety of options. The below mentioned web sites were not chosen arbitrarily but because they stem from different areas: Tiscover from tourism, Immobilien.net from the real estate business and Learn@WU is a distance learning platform. The selection does represent reality very well because the tourism and leisure industry is already one of the most successful areas in e-commerce. According to Marcussen (2006), the overall online travel market size in Europe is increasing continuously during the past years. In 2005, the online travel Internet sales in Europe amounted already to more than 10% of the market and was expected to increase to a share of more than 12% in 2006 (Marcussen, 2006). The e-learning sector is increasingly important and information and communication technologies (ICTs) offer new opportunities for distance learning (Cantoni, Cellario, & Porta, 2004; Ong, Lai, & Wang, 2004). Personalised service is particularly crucial in the e-learning environment (Chen, Lee, & Chen, 2004).

Another reason why these three personalised internet applications were chosen for evaluation is that they have different levels of personalisation and recommendation services. The degree of personalisation addresses the issue of how much the results can be tailored to the particular preferences and constraints of the user. For the online real estate platform the level of personalisation was the highest because there are numerous possibilities and functionalities to specify preferences and constraints. Tiscover, the travel web site enables the user to get a quite good amount of personalisation by offering extended search functions. Finally, the level of personalisation of Learn can be classified as low to medium depending on which functions the students are using.

Furthermore, the degree of risk involved and the personal effort when using the particular site is likely to be different. The level of risk is typically very high for the travel application since the products and services have high value for the customer but are rather intangible. The degree of risk for the real estate platform is considered to be medium to high because real estate are of high value as well but they can be visited before they are purchased. The degree of risk for Learn@WU is classified as low because often it is used as simple information providing tool not really suggesting items out of different alternatives. Another reason why these particular internet applications were chosen is the varying level of complexity. The level of complexity could be very high or medium for the travel and the real estate internet application depending on the task. The level of complexity is lower for Learn@WU because it is rather easy to get an overview which tasks can be performed at the web site and the number of available tasks is limited.

Table 11. Classification of the Personalised Internet Applications Tested

Personalised Internet Application	Level of Personalisation	Degree of Risk	Complexity
Tiscover	Medium-High	High	Medium - High
Immobilien.net	High	Medium - High	Medium - High
Learn@WU	Low-Medium	Low	Low - Medium

The following sub-sections will describe the respective personalised internet applications in greater detail. Furthermore, the reasons why particularly they were chosen for the evaluation are outlined.

4.3.1 Tiscover

Tiscover is a travel website offering information and/or online booking of separate parts of a travel i.e. accommodation or activity. Furthermore, complete travel bundles can be booked as well. The travel and leisure industry was an obvious candidate to be represented in this study because travel products and services receive rising attention on the WWW (Marcussen, 2006).

Why was the personalised internet application Tiscover chosen among all the online travel platforms? The web site provides advanced booking functions offering recommendation as well. Often, the possibilities to express interests, preferences and constraints are very limited with other systems (e.g. www.expedia.de, www.lastminute.com or www.allesreise.com). On the Tiscover web site many details can be specified and there is a great variety of interests among which the user can express his or her preferences and activities to be pursued during the vacation.

4.3.2 Learn@WU

The second PIA is Learn@WU (https://learn.wu-wien.ac.at/), the e-learning platform of the Vienna University of Economics and Business Administration (VUEBA). The platform has recently been re-developed, improved and offers now the possibility for the students to personalise the interface. Students are increasingly using the opportunity to have an e-learning web site tailored to their respective courses and exams they are taking.

4.3.3 Immobilien.net

Immobilien.net is an online real estate platform on which real estate agencies can post their offers and users can search for real estates. This website was chosen because the searching functions are very extensive. Thus, the degree of personalisation can be very high if the customer is using the functions allowing tailoring proposals to his or her individuals' preferences and constraints.

4.4 Study Participants

The study participants asked to evaluate the specific internet applications were recruited in different ways. Students of the Vienna University of Economics and Business Administration (VUEBA) were invited to participate in the survey about Learn@WU. Several ways were applied to promote the survey and convince the students to participate in the survey. First, a pop-up was used at the web site Learn@WU to draw students' attention to the survey. Second, it was announced on the web site Learn@WU as well. Furthermore, a lottery served as an incentive for the students to participate in the study. Cinema vouchers were raffled among all students completing the survey and wishing to participate in the lottery.

Various announcements were done for the immobilien.net survey. First, an invitation to participate in the survey was sent to all e-mail addresses subscribed to the newsletter of immobilien.net. Second, the survey was announced at the immobilien.net web site. Third, two partner web sites of immobilien.net (www.job.at, www.partner.at) promoted the survey as well by means of banners. The incentive used for the immobilien.net survey was a raffle of furniture vouchers.

The survey of Tiscover was done in a similar way to the immobilien.net survey. All subscribers of the Tiscover newsletter got the invitation to answer the questionnaire about Tiscover. Furthermore, the survey was announced by banner advertisements at the web sites of www.partner.at and www.job.at. Finally, the survey was sent via a snowball system to friends and relatives.

4.5 Experimental setting and data collection method

For the purpose of creating some degree of situational involvement for each of the personalised internet applications a pre-determined task was proposed. The test task was intended to mimic real problem solving, e.g. to simulate travel planning in the case of Tiscover, to prepare an exam with Learn@WU or to be recommended on a real estate search with Immobilien.net. At the same time sufficient degrees of freedom were kept to allow the test users to organise their web site visit how they liked and to navigate freely.

Test persons were asked to conduct the test task first and to continue with the answering of the questionnaire. The main body of questions included the items used for the research model. Questions about demographics and internet experience concluded the questionnaire. The respective tasks for each web site are outlined in Table 12. The German version of the questionnaire is found in the appendix.

The questionnaire itself and the respective constructs and questions were operationalised by pre-studies as already outlined. The survey was conducted with an online questionnaire tool (CIW by Sawtooth Software http://www.sawtoothsoftware.com/). The rows of the questionnaire were automatically randomised within the dimensions. The time taken for the realisation of the test task and the answering of the questionnaire was 15 minutes on average.

Table 12. Test Tasks for the Respective Internet Applications

Personalised Internet Application	Task
Immobilien.net	Imagine you want to move to another apartment within the next year. You prefer a rental apartment of 70m² which should be located in Vienna preferably in the districts 3.-9. The monthly rent should not exceed 600 Euro. Please look now for an apartment at the web site www.immobilien.net.

Personalised Internet Application	Task
Tiscover	Imagine you want to go on a one week holiday with a friend to Tyrol in September or October. You will travel to the destination by car or train. The total amount for the accommodation should not exceed Euro 1000 for both of you including breakfast. You would like to stay in a hotel with 3 stars at least. You can choose the date of the travel on your own. Now please open the web site www.tiscover.at and search for the accommodation (without booking).
Learn@WU	Imagine you want to attend the "Marketing I" exam at the Vienna University of Economics and Business Administration soon. Therefore, you want to get an overview of the exam with the help of the e-learning system Learn@WU. Now please open the web site https://learn.wu-wien.ac.at. Search for all relevant and interesting information concerning that exam.

5 EMPIRICAL RESULTS

This chapter consists of three major parts. First, descriptive results for the sample are presented and a comparison of the three personalised internet applications is conducted. Second, the structural equation modelling approach and its results are outlined for the total sample as well as for the sub-samples. Third, the method of expert interviews employed in this study is described and results are documented.

5.1 Descriptive Statistics

The descriptive statistics section includes the demographic description of the sample. Furthermore, the personal characteristics for the sample such as experience with the internet and attitude are outlined. Finally, the respective constructs are analysed descriptively to get an impression of how each of the respective areas, e.g. ease of use, satisfaction were evaluated.

Since various incentives were used to attract the attention of potential test persons there is the danger that some test persons completed the questionnaire just for the sake of winning one of the incentives. Therefore, the answers were checked for outliers to avoid that such cases are included in the final sample. The questionnaire contained one question formulated negatively ("The structure of the web site is confusing") belonging to the domain ease of use. This question was primarily used to discover datasets which were not based on serious answers (meaning people were participating in the survey just because they want to win a prize in the raffle and did not care which answer they gave). First, it was checked if people show some different answering behaviour between the positive formulated questions belonging to ease of use ("Overall, I find this web site easy to use", "This web site is user-friendly", "Learnability") and the fourth negative question. If not, the other questions were examined as well looking for inconsistencies. If it was detected that the negative formulated question was answered inconsistently (answered positively although the others were answered positive as well) and the others seem to be answered without really thinking about the web site too (e.g. the answers were mainly "I totally agree" or "I do not agree at all" regardless of the questions) those cases were excluded from further analysis. Furthermore, cases were excluded from the analysis if a respondent seemed to answer just the same or nearly the same for all of the questions. However, this issue was not a big problem and only 4 cases were deleted from the final sample. Moreover, incomplete questionnaires were excluded as well if questions focussing on the constructs were not answered. Incomplete questionnaires were included if only demographic answers or provider specific answers (questions the web site providers wanted to add) were missing. Finally, the total sample size included 1386 completed questionnaires as outlined in Table 13.

Table 13. Sample Size

Web Site	Sample Size
Learn@WU	727
Immobilien.net	422
Tiscover	237
Total	**1386**

5.1.1 Demographic Description of the Sample

This sub-section is intended to give an overview of how the sample is composed. Table 14 presents the results for the gender distribution and how the various age groups are represented in the study at hand. Furthermore, the current profession and education is indicated (see Table 14).

As far as the distribution of gender is concerned, more female (56%) than male respondents (44%) participated in the survey. The sample can be classified as rather young with more than 60% being below 30 years.

Row 3 in Table 14 outlines the education levels of the respondents. More than 60% of the test persons have A-levels, followed by 15% who completed either an apprenticeship or a vocational school. Almost 20% of the respondents have a university or university of applied sciences degree. As far as the current profession of the study participants is concerned, the majority of the sample are students followed by employed persons and self-employed persons. For the demographic questions cases with missing values were accepted. Therefore, the sum in Table 14 does not always amount exactly to 100% of the sample.

Table 14. Demographic Characteristics of Respondents (N=1386)

Demographic Characteristics	Frequencies	
	Absolute	Relative
Gender		
- Female	775	56%
- Male	609	44%
Age		
- 18-30	848	61.2%
- 31-40	238	17.2%
- 41-50	167	12.1%
- 51 and more	106	7.6%
Education		
- University	188	13.6%
- University of applied sciences	75	5.4%
- A-levels	886	64.0%
- Apprenticeship or vocational school	207	15.0%
- Compulsory Education	22	1.6%
Profession		
- Employed	440	31.8%
- Self-employed	106	7.7%
- Student	782	49.3%
- Retiree	40	2.9%
- Housewife/Houseman	27	2%
- Miscellaneous	85	6.1%

5.1.2 Personal Characteristics of the Sample

Further personal characteristics of the sample covered by the study are the attitude towards information search via the Internet and WWW experience or familiarity. Results for both of the constructs seem to be very positive. The test persons were quite experienced and the attitude towards information search via the WWW is positive.

5.1.2.1 WWW Usage and Experience

Two questions were used to find out how the general WWW experience of the test persons is. A third question aimed to investigate the test person's knowledge of the particular web site. Figure 14 describes how often the respondents use the WWW on the average. Nearly, three quarters use it daily, another 19% use it several times a week, the others less often.

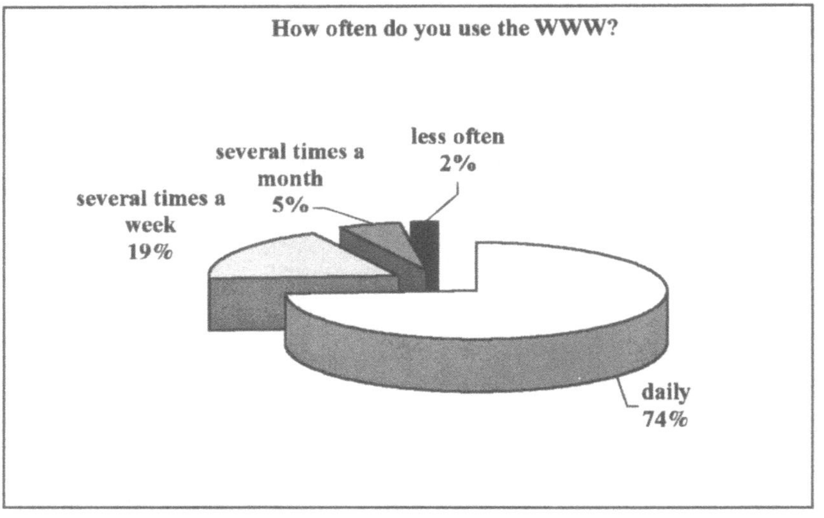

Figure 14. Average Use of the WWW

The next question focused on the self-assessment of the test persons of how experienced they are when interacting with the WWW. This additional question was applied because the frequency of usage itself does not give any cue of how confident persons are when browsing the Web. The results show that the majority sees themselves as experienced. A little bit less than one half of the test persons consider themselves as being a very experienced user (see Table 15).

Table 15. Self-assessment of WWW Experience

Do you consider yourself as an experienced WWW user?	Frequencies	
	Absolute	Relative
Very experienced	624	45.1%
Experienced	676	48.8%
Less experienced	73	5.3%
Not experienced	11	0.8%

The final experience question was related to the knowledge of the particular personalised internet application (Figure 15).

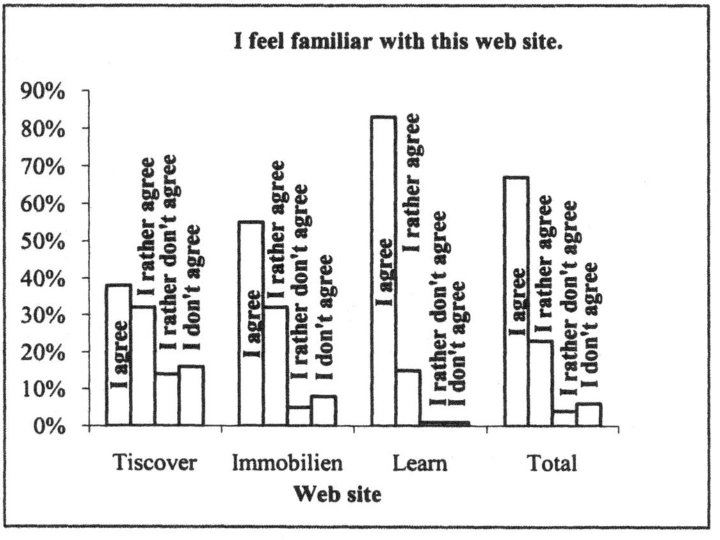

Figure 15. Self-assessment of Web Site Familiarity

The question outlined in Figure 15 was intended to capture the respondents' familiarity with the web site. This self-assessment question was chosen because asking how often they have used it would be problematic because the web site visits could be very short ones or could have taken place already a long time ago. Such a question would say nothing about the familiarity with the web site.

The statement was "I am familiar with the web site because of previous visits." Overall (for the whole sample), 66.5% felt very familiar with the web site, 23.4% being rather familiar. 10% of the respondents were rather not familiar or not familiar at all. Figure 15 shows the difference between the respective internet applications. Obviously, the familiarity differs for the three personalised internet applications. Learn is by far the system test persons were most familiar with followed by Immobilien. The web site Tiscover has with 30% the highest rate of being non-familiar or rather non-familiar among the respondents.

5.1.2.2 Attitude towards online information search

Overall the attitude of the respondents indicates that they consider information search via the WWW as being useful.

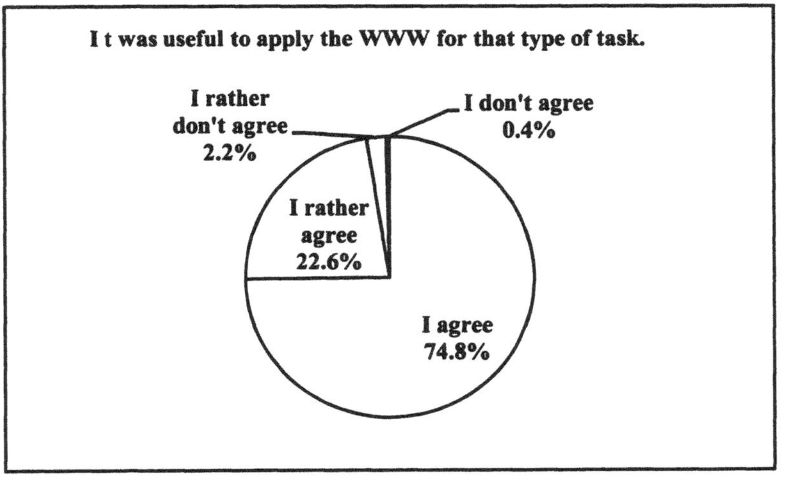

Figure 16. The Usefulness of the WWW for the Task

Three quarters of the test persons found the use of the Web helpful to solve the given task (see Figure 16). Only 25% of the respondents agreed that search via WWW is too time-consuming.

For the question "I found it useful to obtain information about real estate/ travel/ learning material via the WWW." it makes sense to have a separate look on the results for each of the web sites. Figure 17 shows that there are no main differences. However, the Learn@WU respondents found it most useful with nearly 80% agreeing on that question. The agreement of Immobilien.net test persons was high as well (74.5%); however it was the lowest level of agreement compared to the other two web sites.

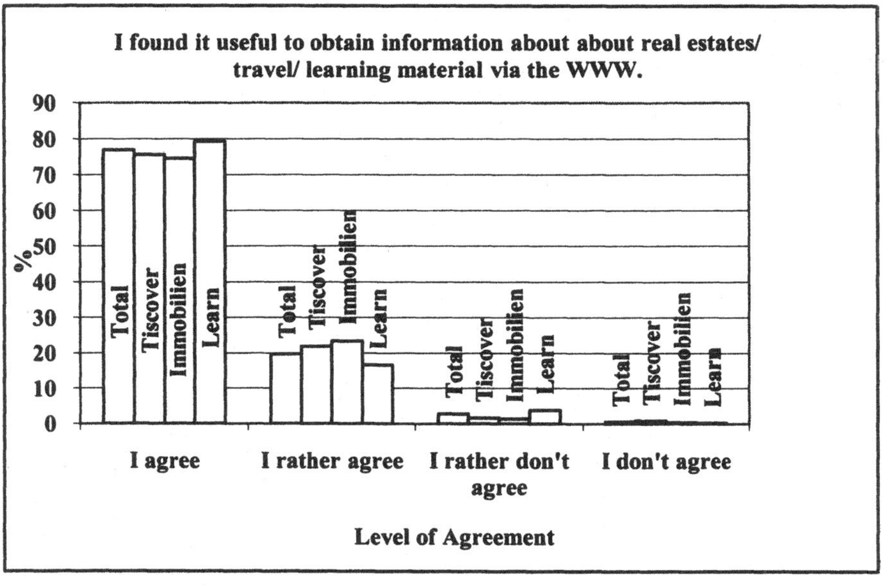

Figure 17. Usefulness of Obtaining Information via the WWW

5.1.3 Comparison of the three Personalised Internet Applications

Some descriptive construct analysis - an overview of how the respective constructs ease of use, usefulness, trust and exploratory behaviour were perceived by the respondents is given in the following section. The outcome, i.e. satisfaction and commitment will be described descriptively as well. Moreover, a comparison of the three systems will be realised.

5.1.3.1 Ease of Use

Table 16 shows the items for the construct ease of use. Overall, the results for ease of use were satisfactory with each question being agreed or rather agreed on an 80% level. The question about the structure of the web site being formulated negatively was disagreed with 80%.

Table 16. Items for the Construct "Ease of Use"

"Ease of Use"
• Overall, I find this web site easy to use.
• This web site is user friendly.
• It is easy to learn how to use the web site by new users.
• The structure of the web site is confusing.

The first ease of use question received the most positive answer in the total sample. 52.5% of the respondents agreed that the web site was easy to use. Almost 40% answered this question with I rather agree. Only 6.8 did rather not agree and slightly more than one percent disagreed. Table 17 presents the differences among the three web sites. Obviously, Tiscover received worse results for this question with only 43.5% of total agreement. Almost 15% rather not agreed and this is the highest level of disagreement for that question compared among the three web sites.

Table 17. Overall Ease of Use

Level of agreement	Personalised Internet Application		
	Tiscover	Immobilien	Learn
I agree	43.5%	53.2%	55.2%
I rather agree	40.1%	39.2%	39.5%
I rather don't agree	14.3%	6.1%	4.7%
I don't agree	2.1%	1.4%	0.7%

What are the results for the second item "This web site is user friendly"? The average result was slightly worse than for the first question with 49.4% totally agreeing that the web site is user friendly. However, the percentage of respondents who rather agreed was with 44.4 higher than for the first question.

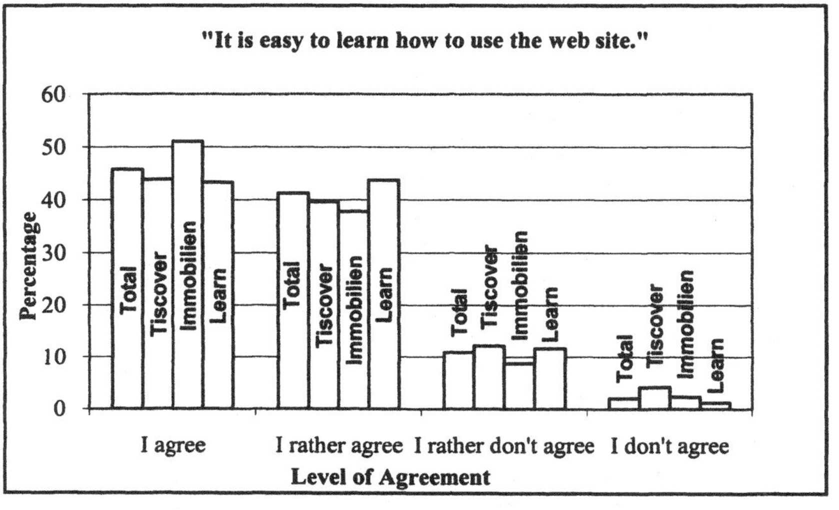

Figure 18. Learnability of the Web Sites

Another question was concerned with the test persons' opinion if new users can easily learn how to use the web site. The results were surprising for this question as the average outcome for the three systems applies more or less for Tiscover and Learn@WU as well. However, the web site www.immobilien.net is positively salient with nearly 90% of the test persons being convinced that it is easy to learn how to use the web site (see Figure 18).

The last question of the construct ease of use referred to the structure of the personalised internet applications. This statement was formulated negatively to check the respondents' attention as outlined in Section 5.1. 80% of the test persons disagreed, the disagreement was with 73% lower for Tiscover then for the other two web sites (Immobilien: 79% and Learn@WU 84%). Next, a closer look is taken on the construct of usefulness.

5.1.3.2 Usefulness

Usefulness being another indispensable characteristic of a web site is analysed in greater detail. This construct was measured with four items as indicated in Table 18.

Table 18. Items for the Construct "Usefulness"

"Usefulness"
• Overall, I find this web site being useful.
• The use of Learn@WU / immobilien.net / Tiscover did facilitate my search for learning materials / real estate / a travel.
• This web site enables me to quickly find interesting information.
• This web site is increasing the quality of my information search.

As far as the first question is concerned the composite usefulness (for all three web sites) is perceived by 68% as definitely useful. 29% of the test persons rather agreed (Table 19).

When it comes to look at the three web sites separately, there are no big differences regarding the agreement and the disagreement. However, a distinction can be drawn when looking at the respondents indicating that they fully agree compared to those who rather agree. The web site Learn@WU is by far the one which is perceived to be most useful with 80% fully agreeing. Table 19 further outlines the differences among the web sites for this question of usefulness.

Table 19. Usefulness of the Web Sites

Level of agreement	**Personalised Internet Application**			
	Tiscover	Immobilien	Learn	Total
I agree	48.1%	58.4%	80.7%	68.3%
I rather agree	46.8%	38.5%	17.6%	29.0%
I rather don't agree	4.2%	1.4%	1.5%	1.9%
I don't agree	0.8%	1.7%	0.1%	0.7%

The answers to the second question were more differentiated across each web site. Learn@WU was obviously the web site being perceived very useful for the search of learning materials. Surprisingly, this time it was immobilien.net which got the worst evaluation (see Figure 19). However, this could be due to the fact that the online based search for real estate is not that widespread as it is for the travel sector or for learning materials.

Another item was concerned with the time frame – how quickly can the desired piece of information be found on the web site? At least 80% of the respondents agreed or rather agreed that they found useful information within a time being perceived by them as quick. Learn@WU and www.immobilien.net are performing better than Tiscover (with 19% disagreement for that question compared to 7% of Immobilien and 9% of Learn@WU).

The last question of usefulness refers to the quality of information search. The same picture shows up like for the previous question. The overall satisfaction with the quality of information search is about 90% but lower for the web site Tiscover with only 82%.

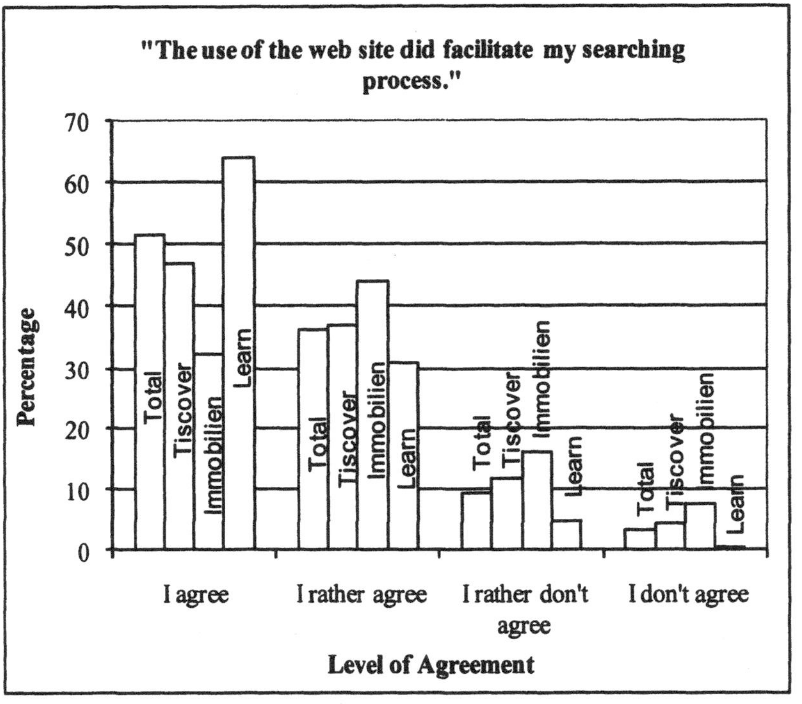

Figure 19. Facilitation of the Searching Process through Online Resources

The weaker results of Tiscover when compared to the other two web sites have to be put into perspective because the three personalised internet applications which were evaluated have different positions on the market. Learn@WU has a quasi-monopoly position because students studying at the Vienna University of Economics and Business Administration have no other choice if they want to use online learning material. The only option is to use conventional materials like offline books or scripts. In contrast, the competition for online real estate platforms is higher. When it comes to travel there are even more web sites being potential competitors. Furthermore, the assumption arises that different characteristics have distinctive significance for the respective sectors. For some web sites like an e-learning platform it is most important to be useful whereas for the travel sector trust and fun might have greater significance. However, this assumption will be tested and outlined in the section on Structural

Equation Modelling where the influences on satisfaction are analysed for each personalised internet application.

5.1.3.3 Enjoyment

Next, a totally different area is the subject: the construct of perceived enjoyment. Enjoyment is serving as a competing construct to exploratory browsing behaviour. It is hypothesised that the construct of exploratory browsing behaviour is the more appropriate one in the context of personalised internet applications. This is going to be tested in the section on Structural Equation Modelling.

Table 20. Items for the Construct "Enjoyment"

"Enjoyment"
• This web site induces new ideas.
• This web site enhances my creativity.
• This web site arouses my imagination.

Surprisingly, the positive results for the first question of enjoyment completely favour the travel web site Tiscover. More than 60% of the respondents agreed that the use of the web site creates new ideas in the case of Tiscover. Only 53% of the test persons thought that they created new ideas when using the web site www.immobilien.net. Learn@WU got 32% positive answers.

The second question of enjoyment "This web site enhances my creativity" reflects a similar picture, though differences among the web sites are not that strong. The average agreement amounts to 30%, Tiscover got 38% positive consent for that question, Immobilien.net even 40% and Learn@WU achieved 22% agreement of the respondents. Finally, when it comes to evaluate if the web site made the test persons feel imaginative, results are rather balanced except for Learn.

Table 21. Does the Web Site Create New Ideas?

Level of agreement	Personalised Internet Application			
	Tiscover	Immobilien	Learn	Total
I agree	24.1%	18.4%	6.2%	13.0%
I rather agree	37.1%	34.3%	25.7%	30.3%
I rather don't agree	29.5%	34.8%	51.4%	42.6%
I don't agree	9.3%	12.5%	16.6%	14.1%

A competing construct which is hypothesised to perform better than enjoyment when applying to personalised internet applications is exploratory browsing behaviour outlined in the following sub-chapter.

5.1.3.4 Exploratory Browsing Behaviour

Exploratory Browsing Behaviour which deals a lot with inspiration, novelty seeking, variety seeking and curiosity is hypothesised to be more appropriate because personalised internet applications should induce exploratory browsing more than ordinary web sites. They should present personalised results very soon to the user. Therefore, after having found appropriate proposals the user can move on with exploratory browsing, e.g. to find additional information on financing in the case of real estate or journey and infrastructure information in the case of the travel web site. Furthermore, the concept of exploratory browsing goes beyond just being a "fun" web site.

Table 22. Items for the Construct "Exploratory Browsing Behaviour"

"Exploratory Browsing Behaviour"
• The visit of the web site offered me variety.
• This web site inspired me.
• This web site excited my curiosity.

"Exploratory Browsing Behaviour"
• The use of the web site was exciting to me.
• The web site offered novel information / products to me.
• Using the web site was a pleasure.

For the first question, one quarter of the respondents agreed that the respective web site offered some variety. 43% of the test persons rather agreed and the rest of 32% did not or rather did not agree.

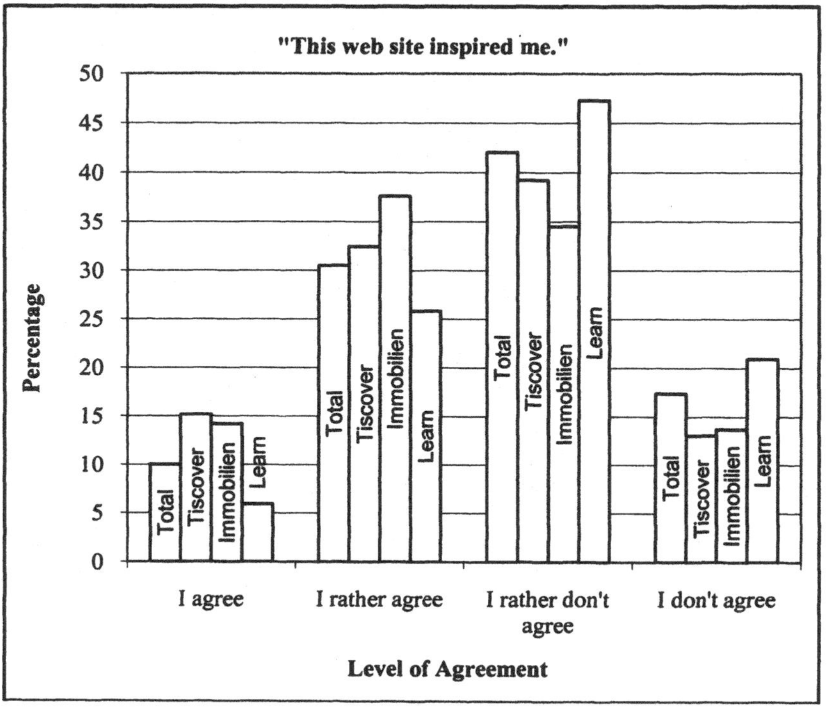

Figure 20. Inspiration of the Web Sites

The second question ("This web site inspired me.") showed some major differences when analysing the web sites separately. Although, the general agreement upon the inspiring function of the three web sites was not very high the perceived inspiration was higher for the web sites Immobilien.net and Tiscover. Both of them offer some inspiring content, additional information such as a guide or weather at www.tiscover.at or information about furniture or financing on the real estate web site. Nearly one half of the respondents agreed in the case of Tiscover and slightly more than one half for Immobilien.net while for Learn@WU it was just 32% of agreement. Certainly, this can be due to the fact that Learn@WU is rather used for goal directed purposes.

The question dealing with curiosity responding functions of the web site showed a similar picture like the previous question. Although being rated better than the inspiration question, Tiscover and Immobilien.net got better results than Learn@WU. Again, this is certainly due to the different purposes of the web sites.

As far as the question "The web site offered novel information / products to me." is regarded, the results turn in favour of Learn@WU receiving the best ratings with a level of agreement of more than 83% (compared to only 67% of Tiscover and 79% of Immobilien).

Table 23. Novelty of Information or Products

Level of agreement	Personalised Internet Application			
	Total	Immobilien	Learn	Tiscover
I agree	30.8%	28.4%	34.0%	25.3%
I rather agree	48.3%	50.1%	49.5%	41.8%
I rather don't agree	16.9%	16.5%	14.4%	24.9%
I don't agree	4.0%	5.0%	2.1%	8.0%

When looking at the overall ratings of the exploratory browsing behaviour questions it becomes evident that the inspiration question received the worst evaluations (see Table 24). The same turns out when the exploratory browsing behaviour assessments for all three personalised internet applications are regarded.

Table 24. Overall Ratings for Exploratory Browsing Behaviour Items

Level of Agreement	Question					
	Variety	Inspiration	Curiosity	Excitement	Novelty	Pleasure
I agree	24.8%	10.0%	20.9%	17.2%	30.8%	18.8%
I rather agree	42.9%	30.5%	42.2%	38.6%	48.3%	48.9%
I rather don't agree	25.7%	42.1%	29.5%	34.4%	16.9%	25.9%
I don't agree	6.6%	17.4%	7.4%	9.8%	4.0%	6.4%

The other Exploratory Browsing Behaviour items got a level of agreement of approximately 60% except excitement which got positive ratings of 55.8%. Novelty-seeking was by far the item receiving best ratings with 79% of the respondents agreeing that the web site offered novel products or information. The second most popular items were variety and pleasure being rated positively by 68%. Next, the focus is upon a serious subject not related to fun and hedonic motivations at all – the issue of trust.

5.1.3.5 Trust

The final construct of the independent, exogenous constructs is trust which is hypothesised to be substantial considering the ongoing and increasing internet fraud cases and caveats. Table 25 displays the items used to measure trust.

Overall, the construct of trust is rated good because the level of disagreement is not exceeding 20% for none of the items. Another recurring result is that Learn@WU is almost always assessed best in terms of trust and security standards when compared to the other two.

Table 25. Items for the Construct "Trust"

"Trust"
• This web site conveys the feeling that personal information is treated confidentially.
• I trust the information indicated on the web site.
• I have the impression that the web site www.immobilien.net / https://learn.wu-wien.ac.at / www.tiscover.at is secure.
• The web site seems like being equipped with the best security standards.
• The proposals (searching results) of the web site were convincing.

If a closer look is taken at the results for trust, the question referring to trust towards information is evaluated best. Learn@WU is by far the one being assessed most positively with more than 95% agreement (compared to almost 90% of Immobilien.net and Tiscover) as shown in Figure 21.

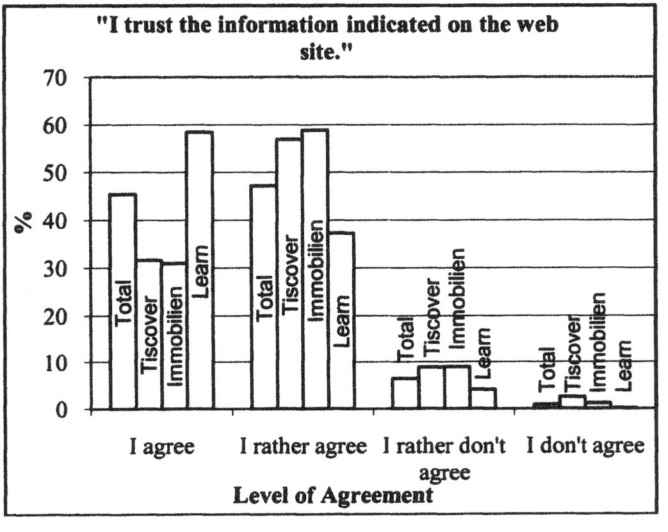

Figure 21. Trust towards the Information

The worst average results as well as web site specific results were received for the question about security standards presented in Table 26.

Table 26. Perceived Security Standards

"The web site seems like being equipped with the best security standards."				
Level of agreement	**Personalised Internet Application**			
	Total	**Tiscover**	**Immobilien**	**Learn**
I agree	22.7%	16.9%	19.4%	26.4%
I rather agree	59.8%	63.3%	61.2%	57.9%
I rather don't agree	15.1%	14.3%	16.5%	14.4%
I don't agree	2.5%	5.5%	2.8%	1.2%

If the question is formulated a bit less rigorous or detailed with "I have the impression that the web site www.immobilien.net / https://learn.wu-wien.ac.at / www.tiscover.at is secure." the results are slightly better. Only 9% of the respondents disagreed (or rather disagreed) on average (13% for Tiscover, 10% for Immobilien and 8% for Learn@WU). If the test persons were asked about their impression that personal information is treated confidentially at the respective web sites, the majority answered the question positively. However, 15% of the total sample did not have the impression of the confident treatment of personal information. The disagreement was highest for Tiscover with 18% followed by Learn with 14% and Immobilien.net with 13% of the respondents answering negatively.

The last and very interesting question was concerned with the trustworthiness of the proposals and searching results given by the system. The best result was reached by Immobilien.net with 94% agreeing (compared to 87% of Tiscover and 84% of Learn).

The following section is taking a close look on the dependent and endogenous variables of the study. First, satisfaction is analysed and compared across the web sites. Second, the results for commitment (if the web site will be recommended to others and if it will be used again) are outlined.

5.1.3.6 Satisfaction

The construct of satisfaction was measured with five items covering different facets of satisfaction like expectations or experiences with the web sites (see Table 27). A 4-point Likert scale from I agree to I don't agree like for the previous questions was applied. Furthermore, there was one question serving as an overall measurement item asking about general satisfaction with the web site. For this question the answering possibilities were "I am very satisfied", "I am rather satisfied", "I am rather not satisfied" and "I am not satisfied at all".

Table 27. Items for the Construct "Satisfaction"

"Satisfaction"
• I am satisfied with the outcome of my information search.
• Overall, I made some positive experiences with the use of Learn @WU / www.immobilien.net / www.tiscover.at.
• The quality of the proposals / searching results was convincing.
• This web site meets my expectations.
• Overall, how is your impression of this web site? (global satisfaction item)

First, the global satisfaction will be analysed to gain insight how the satisfaction with the web sites was rated overall by respondents. Figure 22 outlines that the satisfaction level for all three of the systems is generally quite good with an agreement level of at least 87%. The total average satisfaction is with 94% of the respondents very high and the majority is even very satisfied (44% being rather satisfied).

Best results were achieved with the question about experiences with the web site being almost 90% overall as well as if the web sites are analysed individually (Table 28). Learn@WU got the best ratings with only 3% of the respondents indicating that they rather did not have a good experience with the web site.

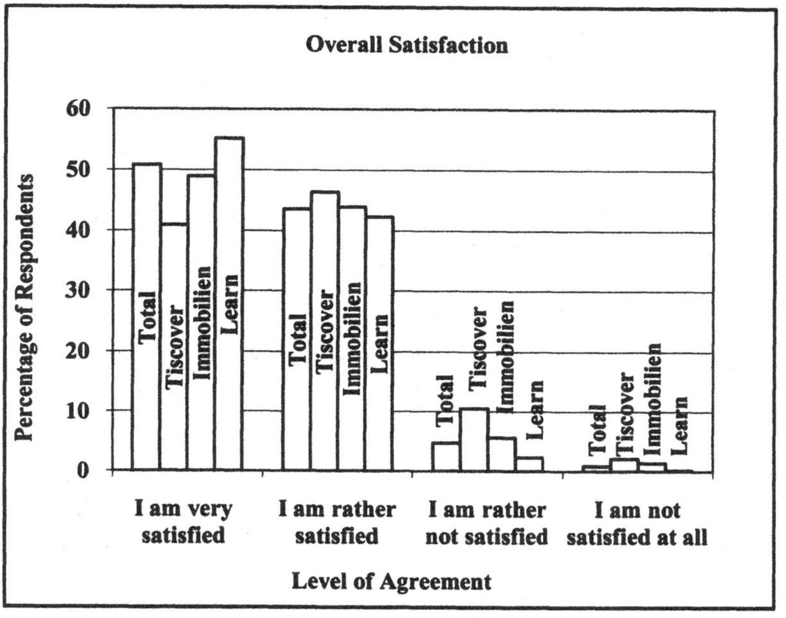

Figure 22. Overall, how is your Impression of this Web Site?

Worst ratings were given to the question about the satisfaction with proposals and searching results. Overall, 81% of the test persons were satisfied (23%) or rather satisfied (58%). Immobilien.net achieved best ratings with 84% being satisfied. However, when looking at the percentages of dissatisfaction it is Learn which got the best results for the answering category of "I am not satisfied at all" with only 0.8% agreeing (compared to 3.3% of Immobilien and 6.3% of Tiscover).

As far as the results for the question "This web site meets my expectations." are regarded rather different ratings arose. The overall agreement was 88%, for Learn@WU it was even 92%. Immobilen.net achieved 88% of agreement among the respondents. In the case of Tiscover, 78% of the study participants' expectations were met.

Finally, what about the outcome of the information search? The best results were obtained for the online learning platform with 42% of the respondents being satisfied with the outcome and 51% being rather satisfied. For

Immobilien.net the percentage of respondents indicating that they were rather satisfied was the same (with 51%). However, the number of test persons who have been very satisfied was lower with 32%. Tiscover got 35% of respondents agreeing to that question and 47% rather agreeing. The final construct described will be commitment which is hypothesised to be determined by satisfaction.

Table 28. Positive Experience with the Web Site

Level of agreement	Personalised Internet Application			
	Total	Tiscover	Immobilien	Learn
I agree	54.5%	33.8%	40.7%	69.3%
I rather agree	38.9%	53.6%	50.4%	27.4%
I rather don't agree	5.6%	9.3%	7.6%	3.2%
I don't agree	1.1%	3.4%	1.4%	0.1%

5.1.3.7 Commitment

Commitment is measured in this study by the intention to revisit the web site as well as whether the respondents plan to recommend the web site to others.

Table 29. Items for the Construct "Commitment"

"Commitment"
• I can recommend this web site.
• I will revisit this web site.
• I will use this web site more often in the future.

The respondents answered most positive to the question about their intention to revisit the web site compared to the other commitment questions. More than 85% of the respondents have the intention to revisit the web site (overall as well as for the respective web sites). However, this has to be put into perspective because among the test persons may be regular users in the case of Tiscover and Immobilien.net and there are certainly regular users of Learn@WU among the respondents. Table 30 shows the detailed answers for this question.

Table 30. Intention to Revisit the Web Site

Level of agreement	Personalised Internet Application			
	Total	Tiscover	Immobilien	Learn
I agree	70.6%	45.1%	63.1%	83.4%
I rather agree	24.6%	41.4%	29.8%	16.1%
I rather don't agree	3.2%	9.3%	4.7%	0.4%
I don't agree	1.5%	4.2%	2.4%	0.1%

When looking at the results for the question about the intention of the respondents to use the web site more often in the future, results got worse. Overall, 83% of the test persons agree or rather agree (72% in the case of Tiscover, 80% for Immobilien.net and 88% for Learn@WU).

The most interesting commitment question was probably if the web site is intended to be recommended to others. Obviously a web site is only recommended if oneself is satisfied with it and if it is found to be useful or enjoyable or fulfils some kind of desired function. Only 2% of the Learn@WU study participants indicated that they would rather not recommend it, for Immobilien the percentage disagreeing with the statement "I would recommend this web site." was 6%, in case of Tiscover 15% disagreed.

The intention of this section was to give an overview of how the respective constructs and questions were answered. The next section concentrates on the analysis of effects of the independent constructs (Usefulness, Ease of Use,

Exploratory Browsing Behaviour and Trust) on the dependent variables satisfaction and commitment.

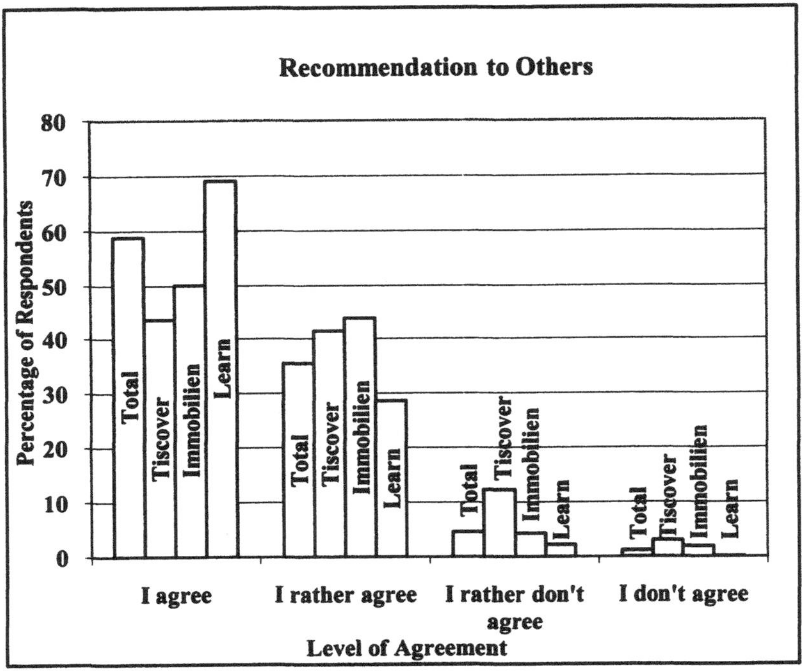

Figure 23. Do you Intend to Recommend the Web Site?

5.2 Testing the Structural Model of Satisfaction with Personalised Internet Applications

The basic goal of this dissertation is to identify relationships between the constructs outlined in previous sections. Structural Equation Modelling (SEM) can handle and explain relationships between latent (unobserved) and manifest (observed) constructs. The modelling technique is a confirmatory rather than an exploratory method. SEM is able to identify causal influences of the exogenous (independent) on the endogenous (dependent) variables. This is similar to regression analysis but has the additional capability to identify the influences of endogenous variables upon one another (Anderson & Gerbing, 1988; Hair,

Anderson, Tatham, & Black, 1998). This study deals with latent constructs (e.g. attitude towards information search via the WWW, trust towards the web site and the processing of information, overall satisfaction with the web site) and proposes hypotheses and relationships between the constructs (outlined in Chapter 3). Therefore, SEM was identified to be the most appropriate analyzing technique. The software program to identify relationships relevant to this study is AMOS. AMOS is an additional module of SPSS, the latest version is 5.0.

Structural equation modelling has a lot of interesting facets and there would be numerous issues to report on. However, only the most important ones (model fit indicators, differentiation between measurement and structural model) and currently discussed topics like formative versus reflective indicators are further outlined in this study. Therefore, this section covers the following topics:

- Formative versus reflective indicators in SEM
- Differentiation between measurement and structural Model
- Model evaluation of SEM and fit indicators
- Results of SEM for this study
- Results of SEM for each of the personalised internet applications by multiple group analysis

5.2.1 Formative versus Reflective Indicators

One crucial distinction which is discussed recently more and more in methodological papers about SEM are formative versus reflective indicators. Are some reflective indicators sometimes used by researchers as if they were formative? Is the difference between the two known enough? Figure 24 and Figure 25 aim to illustrate the difference between the approaches. In a formative measurement model the items are influencing or forming the latent variable. Formative indicators are also known as "cause indicators" (Eggert & Fassott, 2003). They can be seen as exhaustive and an example is the socio-economic status. Indicators like education and income are influencing or causing the latent variable (Chin, 1998). The coefficient "y" represents the weight of the respective indicator to the latent variable. The correlations "r" are illustrated by the two headed arrows.

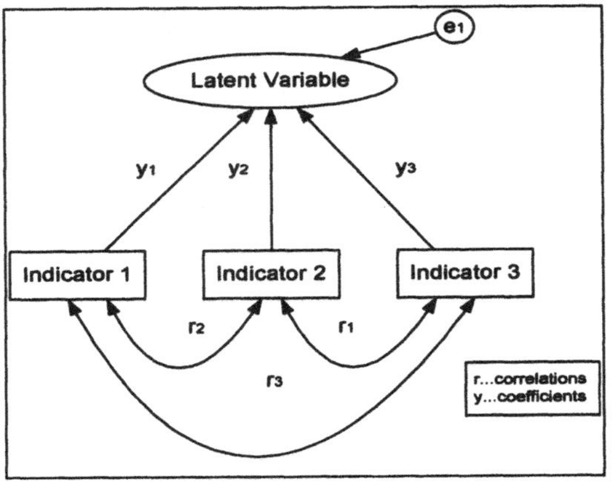

Figure 24. Formative Indicators

The opposite is the case for a reflective measurement model: the latent variable is affecting the respective items (Eggert & Fassott, 2003). The items or indicators (effect indicators) are just an example of how to express the latent construct and could be replaced by other indicators. A change in the latent variable would result in a change of all of the indicators (Backhaus, Erichson, Plinke, & Weiber, 2003). The indicators are an error-prone measurement of the construct. Therefore, the error terms are included in the model for each indicator (Eggert & Fassott, 2003). Thus, they are not exhaustive like formative measures.

The controversial issue is that reflective indicators are often treated like formative ones which causes difficulties like a misleading measurement model and different results (Chin, 1998, Albers and Hildebrandt, 2006, Eggert and Fassott 2003). While formative measurement models were rather neglected in the past they receive more attention now and the development and validation of formative models is increasingly proposed (Diamantopoulos & Winklhofer, 2001). In this study the indicators are reflective measures, they are just an example of how to assess e.g. trust or ease of use. The indicators used could be replaced by others and are not exhaustive. If the latent variable changes the indicators change as well.

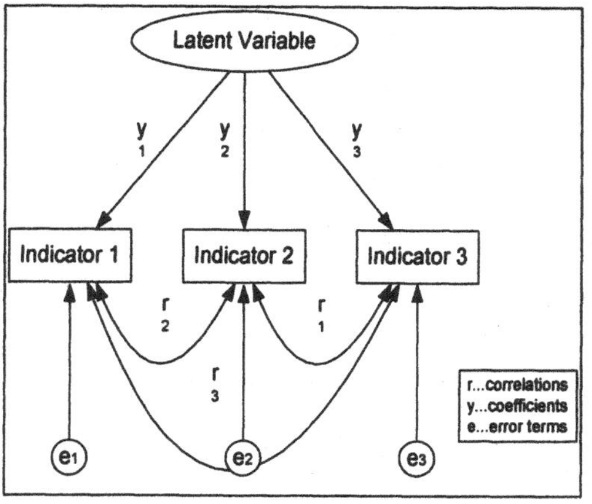

Figure 25. Reflective Indicators

5.2.2 Measurement and Structural Model

The distinction between the measurement and the structural model is another crucial issue when working with SEM. The measurement model describes the relationships between the latent constructs and the indicators. The structural model is concerned with the relations of independent and dependent variables. Figure 26 illustrates these two components, the measurement model being further differentiated between the endogenous (dependent) and the exogenous (independent) constructs. Two different approaches to deal with structural equation modelling are proposed by literature. The first method is to conduct the test of the measurement and structural model simultaneously (Mazanec, 1982). The argument in favour of this approach is that otherwise simple factor analysis and regression analysis could be done. The second approach is relying on a two step procedure. First, the pure measurement model is tested and its model fit is evaluated. Only if fit indices are acceptable the researcher should proceed to test the structural model (Anderson & Gerbing, 1988; Kline, 1998). Both approaches are followed in this study. In fact, the structural equation modelling program AMOS is estimating both models simultaneously. However, the measurement model will be estimated first separately too to gain details about validity and reliability. Next, an overview about different fit indices used in structural equation modelling will be given.

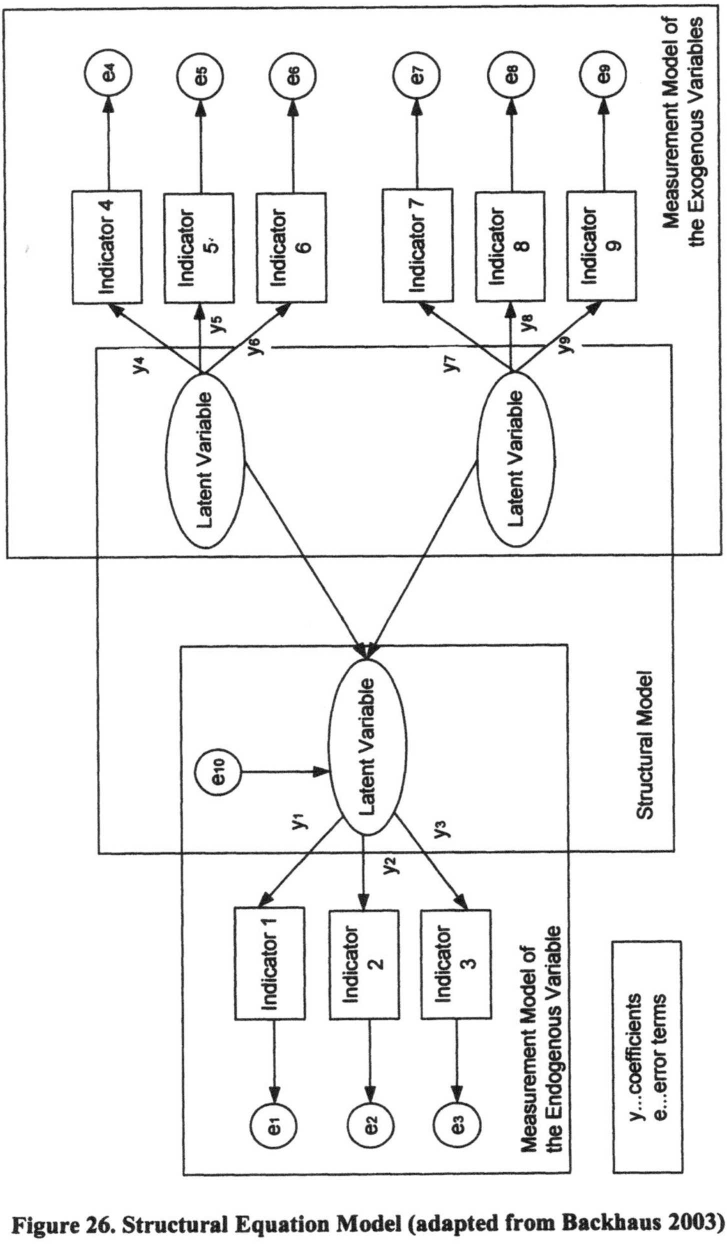

Figure 26. Structural Equation Model (adapted from Backhaus 2003)

5.2.3 Model Evaluation in SEM

Model fits or so called (goodness of) fit indices are reported to evaluate a model. Some rules of thumb found in the literature serve as recommendations. First, the operationalisation is assessed based on the constructs (local measures). For the entire measurement model, the so-called global measures are used for evaluation (Zinnbauer & Eberl, 2004). Finally, the assessment of the structural model is based upon global measures as well.

Fit Measures	
Global Criteria	**Local Criteria**
• Absolute Fit Measures • Incremental Fit Measures • Parsimonious Fit Measures	• Construct Reliability • Convergent Validity • Discriminant Validity

Figure 27. Overview of Categories of Fit Measures (adapted from Zinnbauer and Eberl, 2004)

5.2.3.1 Local Criteria

Local criteria are applied to the measurement model, the operationalisation and the constructs. Fornell and Larcker (1981) proposed that convergent validity, discriminant validity, construct reliability and objectivity should be taken into account. First, some definition of validity and reliability will be given. Reliability is the degree to which the measurement of a variable is burdened with error. However, a variable can never be perfectly measured and a certain measurement error always remains (Backhaus, Erichson, Plinke, & Weiber, 1994; Duncan, 1975; Hair et al., 1998). Are the construct's indicators accurately measuring what they are supposed to measure is a brief explanation of validity (Bollen, 1989; Hair et al., 1998). Although, validity and reliability are interrelated they have to be differentiated: reliability does not imply validity and vice versa (Hair et al., 1998).

Construct reliability, also called composite reliability, is computed with standardised loadings and the measurement error according to the following formula (Hair et al., 1998):

$$\text{Construct Reliability} = \frac{\left(\sum \text{stand.loading}\right)^2}{\left(\sum \text{stand.loading}\right)^2 + \sum \varepsilon_j}$$

As a rule of thumb, construct reliability should be above 0.6 (Bagozzi & Yi, 1988) or even above 0.7 (Hair et al., 1998).

Convergent validity describes the amount of variance covered by the construct compared to the amount of variance which can be allocated to measurement error (Fornell & Larcker, 1981). Convergent validity is assessed with Average Variance Extracted (AVE) or Variance Extracted Measure. It is calculated the way construct reliability is computed except that standardised loadings are squared before they are summed up (Fornell & Larcker, 1981; Hair et al., 1998). The AVE should be greater than 0.5 so that the variance due to measurement error is not higher than the variance captured by the construct (Fornell & Larcker, 1981).

Finally, discriminant validity is the extent to which one construct is differentiating from other concepts for which no theoretical relationship is given (Diamantopoulos & Schlegelmilch, 1997). It can be assessed by comparing AVE and the shared variance between the construct and all other variables in the model. AVE should exceed this difference to meet the requirements of discriminant validity (Fornell & Larcker, 1981).

5.2.3.2 Global Criteria

Global fit measures can be divided into three groups: absolute, incremental (or relative or comparative) and parsimony oriented fit measures. Absolute fit measures evaluate to which degree the structural or measurement model is predicting the observed covariance matrix, what is the degree of explained variance? Incremental/relative/comparative fit measures compare the proposed model to alternative models. How much differs the research (or target) model from the null (or independence, baseline) model? The null model hypothesises that there are no relationships. Parsimony oriented fit measures are penalising too much complexity in the model (Bollen, 1989; Hair et al., 1998; Norman & Streiner, 2003). Table 31 gives an overview of some recommended fit indices and their rules of thumb.

Table 31. Recommended Model Fits in SEM

Absolute Fit Measures	Definition	Acceptable Level	References
X^2 / df	Ratio between chi-square and degrees of freedom	≤ 5 ≤ 3	(Kline, 1998; Schermelleh-Engel, Moosbrugger, & Müller, 2003)
GFI	Goodness of Fit Index, how well are sample data reproduced, an index for the amount of explained variance and covariance	≥ 0.9	(Baumgartner & Homburg, 1996; Byrne, 2001; Schermelleh-Engel et al., 2003)
RMSEA	Root Mean Square Error of Approximation, Computes average lack of fit per degree of freedom	≤0.05 ≤ 0.08	(Hair et al., 1998; Schermelleh-Engel et al., 2003)
RMR	Root Mean Square Residual, Mean residuals between the observed and predicted covariance	close to 0 => better fit< 0.1	(Bollen, 1989; Marsh, Balla, & McDonald, 1988)

Incremental Fit Measures	Definition	Acceptable Level	Authors
CFI	Comparative Fit Index Fit of the model relative to the null model	> 0.95 close to 1	(Hu & Bentler, 1999; Schermelleh-Engel et al., 2003)
TLI	Tucker Lewis Index Compares models, adjusts for complexity	> 0.9 > 0.95	(Hair et al., 1998; Hu & Bentler, 1999)
NFI	Normed Fit Index Compares chi-squares of the model to the null model	> 0.9	(Backhaus et al., 2003; Norman & Streiner, 2003; Schermelleh-Engel et al., 2003)
Parsimonious Fit Measures	**Definition**	**Acceptable Level**	**Authors**
AGFI	Adjusted Goodness of Fit Index Variant of GFI, adjusted for degrees of freedom	> 0.9 > 0.85	(Norman & Streiner, 2003) (Schermelleh-Engel et al., 2003)
PGFI	Parsimonious Goodness of Fit, Variant of GFI, based on the parsimony of the estimated model	close to 0 => better fit	(Hair et al., 1998)
AIC	Akaike Information Criterion, Adjustment of x^2 for the number of estimated parameters, used to compare models	close to 0 => better fit smaller than AIC for comparison model	(Hair et al., 1998; Schermelleh-Engel et al., 2003)

The recommendations in literature suggest that the Chi-square statistic should never be used isolated because it is sensitive to sample size (Baumgartner & Homburg, 1996; Schermelleh-Engel et al., 2003). Furthermore, complex models are usually favoured by a better chi-square statistic. The second absolute fit measures GFI is again accused to be sensitive to sample size (Marsh et al., 1988). For some indexes more than one acceptable level is indicated and it can be said that in general there is no agreement upon acceptable levels in the research community (e.g. Baumgartner and Homburg, 1996, Schermelleh-Engel, et al., 2003). These rules of thumb should not be taken to rigorous because they are considered quite arbitrary and differ from author to author (Schermelleh-Engel et al., 2003).

5.2.4 Results of Testing the Structural Hypotheses

First, an overview of the fit criteria for the measurement model is given and the measurement model and its constructs and indicators are presented. Then, the focus is on the structural model and its fit indicators.

5.2.4.1 Measurement Model

First, a confirmatory factor analysis (CFA) was undertaken to purify the scale. Finally, 21 of the original 33 items remained for the analysis (enjoyment is not further mentioned because it was not used in the final model and served just as a competing dimension to exploratory browsing behaviour).

Table 32 outlines which of the items were used in the questionnaire and finally in the measurement model. Their abbreviations are indicated as well.

Table 32. Final Scales

Dimen-sion	Exploratory behaviour – Operationalisation	Used in the final measure-ment model	Abbre-viation
Ease of Use	Overall, I find this web site easy to use.	X	EOU1

Dimension	Exploratory behaviour – Operationalisation	Used in the final measurement model	Abbreviation
	This web site is user friendly.	X	EOU2
	It is easy to learn how to use this web site.	X	EOU3
	The structure of the web site is confusing.		EOU4
Usefulness	Overall, I find this web site being useful.	X	U1
	The use of Learn@WU / immobilien.net / Tiscover did facilitate my search for learning materials / real estate / a travel.	X	U2
	This web site enables me to quickly find interesting information.		U3
	This web site is increasing the quality of my information search.	X	U4
Exploratory Browsing Behaviour	The visit of the web site offered me variety.		EBB1
	This web site inspired me.		EBB2
	This web site excited my curiosity.	X	EBB3
	The use of the web site was exciting to me.	X	EBB4
	The web site offered novel information / products to me.		EBB5

Dimension	Exploratory behaviour – Operationalisation	Used in the final measurement model	Abbreviation
	Using the web site was a pleasure.	X	EBB6
Trust	This web site conveys the feeling that personal information is treated confidentially.	X	T1
Trust	I trust the information indicated on the web site.		T2
Trust	I have the impression that the web site www.immobilien.net / https://learn.wu-wien.ac.at / www.tiscover.at is secure.	X	T3
Trust	The web site seems like being equipped with the best security standards.	X	T4
Trust	The proposals (searching results) of the web site were convincing.		T5
Attitude	Information acquisition through the web is too time-consuming.	X	A1
Attitude	Information acquisition via the web is useful.		A2
Attitude	I think it was a good idea to use the web for that type of task.	X	A3
Experience / Internet Familiarity	I feel familiar with the web site because of previous usage.	X	EXP1
Experience / Internet Familiarity	How often do you use the WWW on average?	X	EXP2

Dimension	Exploratory behaviour – Operationalisation	Used in the final measurement model	Abbreviation
	Do you consider yourself as an experienced user of the WWW?		EXP3
Satisfaction	I am satisfied with the outcome of my information search.		SAT1
	Overall, I made some positive experiences with the use of Learn @WU / www.immobilien.net / www.tiscover.at.	X	SAT2
	The quality of the proposals / searching results was convincing.		SAT3
	This web site meets my expectations.	X	SAT4
	Overall, how is your impression of this web site? (global satisfaction item)	X	SAT5
Commitment	I can recommend this web site.	X	COMMIT 1
	I will revisit this web site.	X	COMMIT 2
	I will use this web site more often in the future.		COMMIT 3

The measurement model for the independent constructs is outlined in Figure 28. For each of the latent variables one reference (or indicator) variable is selected were the regression weight is constrained to 1.0. This is done to allow the remaining paths to be estimated. The reference variable which should be chosen to assign the regression weight 1.0 is typically the variable having the highest factor loading on a latent variable. The following measurement model for the independent constructs is only valid for the final structural model. The measurement models for the alternative models will not be further outlined since they are finally not used.

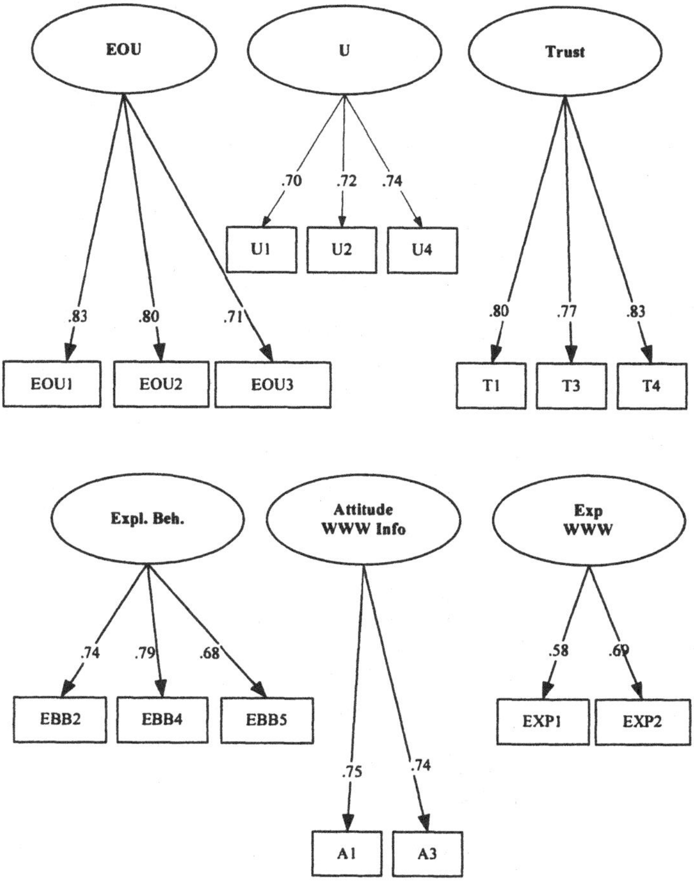

Figure 28. Measurement Model for the Independent Variables

In Figure 29 the measurement model for the dependent variables, satisfaction and commitment is presented with their respective factor loadings.

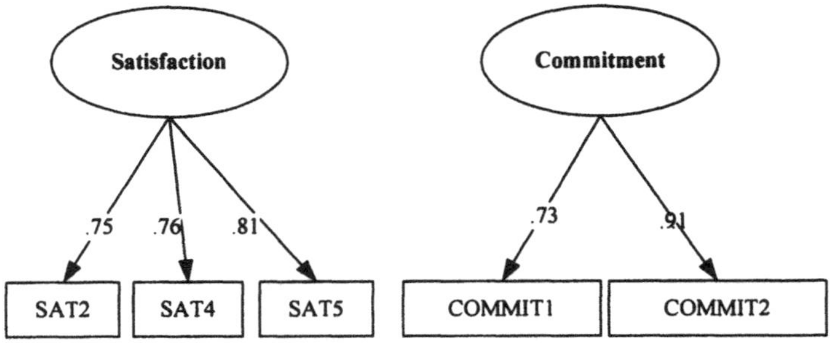

Figure 29. Measurement Model for the Dependent Variables

Next, the local criteria for these items are further outlined and evaluated according to the criteria of reliability and validity.

❖ Local Criteria

First, the operationalisation will be evaluated on a local basis. Factor loadings were already presented in Figure 28 and Figure 29. Next construct reliability, convergent validity (AVE - average variance extracted) and discriminant validity are examined for statistical significance.

Construct Reliability

When looking at construct or composite reliability (see Table 33), all of the constructs met the recommended level of having a reliability above 0.6. Experience is the only negative exception. However, the difference is not a lot below the recommended level missing just 0.02 to achieve 0.6.

All of the variables are related to their constructs at a 0.01 significance level. Furthermore, the indicator reliability can be used as an additional criterion which is recommended to be above 0.4 (Homburg & Baumgartner, 1995). Indicator reliability is the part of the variance of the variable which is explained by the measured variables. This criterion is fulfilled for all of the indicators except one indicator of experience (see Table 33).

Convergent Validity

Average Variance Extracted (AVE) serves as a measure of convergent validity and the recommendation is that it should be above 0.50 so that the variance due to the construct is greater than the variance due to measurement error. For all of the constructs this criterion is fulfilled, except once again for experience.

Table 33. Reliability and Validity of the Constructs

Constructs & Items	Construct Reliability	Indicator Reliability	AVE
Attitude	0.72		0.56
ATT1		0.57	
ATT2		0.55	
Experience	0.58		0.41
EXP1		0.34	
EXP2		0.48	
Exploratory Browsing	0.67		0.55
EXPL1		0.63	
EXPL2		0.46	
EXPL3		0.55	
Trust	0.84		0.64
TRUST1		0.63	
TRUST2		0.69	
TRUST3		0.60	
Usefulness	0.76		0.52
USEFUL1		0.49	
USEFUL2		0.51	
USEFUL3		0.54	
Ease of Use	0.83		0.61

Constructs & Items	Construct Reliability	Indicator Reliability	AVE
EASE1		0.69	
EASE2		0.65	
EASE3		0.51	
Satisfaction	0.82		0.59
SAT2		0.56	
SAT4		0.58	
SAT5		0.66	
Commitment	0.81		0.68
COMMIT1		0.53	
COMMIT2		0.83	

(AVE: Average Variance Extracted)

Obviously, the construct of experience is not performing well when considering construct reliability and average variance extracted. However, when eliminating experience from the measurement model, the global fit criteria (particularly x^2 / df and RMSEA) are significantly getting worse compared to the model proposed in Figure 28. Therefore, it is decided to keep experience in the research model.

Discriminant Validity

Finally, the Fornell and Larcker (1981) approach is applied to assess discriminant validity. AVE should exceed shared variance between the construct and all other constructs which is fulfilled by all of the constructs (except for the shared variance between satisfaction and commitment). Table 34 indicates shared variances which can be compared to AVE in Table 33.

Table 34. Shared Variance to Assess Discriminant Validity

Constructs			Shared Variance
Ease of Use	⇔	Experience	0.00
Ease of Use	⇔	Usefulness	0.51
Ease of Use	⇔	Trust	0.18
Ease of Use	⇔	Attitude	0.05
Ease of Use	⇔	Expl. Browsing	0.16
Usefulness	⇔	Experience	0.02
Usefulness	⇔	Trust	0.24
Usefulness	⇔	Expl. Browsing	0.26
Usefulness	⇔	Attitude	0.20
Trust	⇔	Experience	0.01
Trust	⇔	Expl. Browsing	0.24
Trust	⇔	Attitude	0.04
Expl. Browsing	⇔	Attitude	0.04
Expl. Browsing	⇔	Experience	0.01
Experience	⇔	Attitude	0.26
Satisfaction	⇔	Commitment	0.87

❖ Global Criteria

Table 35 indicates the global fit indices for the measurement model. Not all of the fit indices described above are further outlined because they are redundant and it is not recommended to indicate all of them. When compared to recommended acceptable fit indices as outlined above, all of the indices fulfil these criteria except x^2 / df which is too high depending on the acceptable level one is trusting. However, since the other criteria performed well, the level of x^2 / df is accepted.

Now that global and local fit measures were tested and were found to be acceptable, the structural model will be examined with the goal to confirm or reject the hypothesised relationships.

Table 35. Fit Indices for the Measurement Model

Fit Index	Level
x^2 / df	3.686
GFI	0.969
RMSEA	0.044
NFI	0.959
CFI	0.970
AGFI	0.953

Structural Model

❖ Final Model

First, the final structural model is presented, followed by the fit indices and the outline of the hypotheses being confirmed or rejected. Furthermore, alternative models are tested and separate structural models for each of the personalised internet applications are outlined. All of the path estimates indicated in Figure 30 are significant at a level of 0.001. The insignificant relationships are suppressed in the figure but are outlined in the description below.

The highest influence on satisfaction with the personalised internet applications is attributed to usefulness with a path estimate of 0.56. Therefore, the hypotheses (H1a and H1b) outlined in chapter 3.2 about the direct and indirect influencing factors on satisfaction can be confirmed in the case of usefulness. Usefulness has a strong direct influence (path estimate = 0.56) on satisfaction with the personalised internet application and exerts a strong indirect influence (path estimate = 0.58) via Exploratory Browsing Behaviour. Ease of

Use (EOU) positively affects satisfaction directly (path estimate = 0.19, hypothesis 2a confirmed) as well as indirectly through Usefulness (path estimate = 0.63, hypothesis 2c confirmed) and Trust (path estimate = 0.44, hypothesis 2b confirmed). The only hypothesis relating to trust was that the construct exerts a positive direct influence upon satisfaction. This hypothesis can be confirmed although the influence is not very high with a regression weight of 0.18. The final construct belonging to the category system characteristics is exploratory browsing behaviour which exerts a direct influence upon satisfaction with a regression weight of 0.20, thus confirming hypothesis 4.

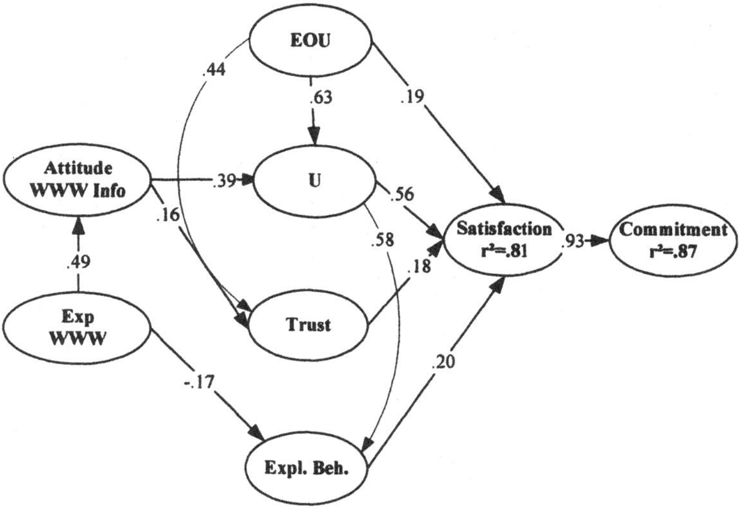

Figure 30. Overall Structural Model Explaining Satisfaction with Personalised Internet Applications

Finally, the hypotheses of the personal characteristics, attitude and internet familiarity are reviewed. Attitude toward information search via the WWW was hypothesised to have a direct influence on satisfaction. This hypothesis (H5a) has to be rejected because the regression weight which is nearly not existent with a path estimate of 0.01 is non-significant (p = 0.754). Hypothesis 5b suggests that attitude affects the level of trust which can be confirmed (path estimate = 0.16). The next hypothesised relationship between attitude and exploratory browsing behaviour has to be rejected (path estimate = 0.04, p = 0.291). Furthermore, attitude has an influence upon usefulness which is quite strong with a regression weight of 0.39 (confirming hypothesis 5d).

Internet familiarity or experience was hypothesised to have several effects: a direct influence on satisfaction and indirect effects via trust, exploratory browsing behaviour, attitude and EOU. The direct influence (hypothesis 6a) on satisfaction is rejected. The regression weight is -0.01 at a p-level of 0.578. Does experience exert an influence on EOU (H6b)? The regression weight is very low with 0.08 and the p level only significant at 0.03. Therefore, this low influence is not further considered in the structural model. Trust is not affected by experience (path estimate = -0.08 and p = 0.196, H6c rejected). Finally, Internet familiarity affects exploratory browsing behaviour negatively (H6d, path estimate = -0.17) and attitude positively (H6e, path estimate = 0.49).

When looking at the fit indices for the structural model, results suggest an excellent fit for incremental fit measures CFI (comparative fit index) and NFI (normed fit index) with both being above 0.95. The same is true for the parsimonious fit measure AGFI (adjusted goodness of fit index) which is highly above the recommended level of 0.9. Finally, the absolute fit measures GFI and RMSEA fulfil the recommended levels of GFI being above 0.9 and RMSEA being below 0.05. Only the ratio of Chi-square to the degrees of freedom is above 3 but below 5.

Table 36. Fit Indices for the Structural Model

Fit Index	Level
X^2 / df	3.716
GFI	0.956
RMSEA	0.044
NFI	0.951
CFI	0.963
AGFI	0.943

❖ Alternative Models

Furthermore, alternative models were tested in which enjoyment was used as a surrogate for exploratory browsing behaviour. Enjoyment is often proposed as an influencing factor for usage, satisfaction or acceptance (e.g. Igbaria et al., 1995, Teo, et al., 1999, Van der Heijden, 2003). Second, another alternative model was proposed by excluding personal factors from the model because the influence of experience and attitude towards online information search and e-services is expected to diminish more and more. A rising number of people are using the Internet on a regular basis and it is increasingly common to search, buy and book online. Furthermore, a lot of studies do not consider these influencing factors when assessing influences on satisfaction, usage or other outcome criteria (e.g. Kim and Stoel, 2004, Shih, 2004, Hsu and Chiu, 2003).

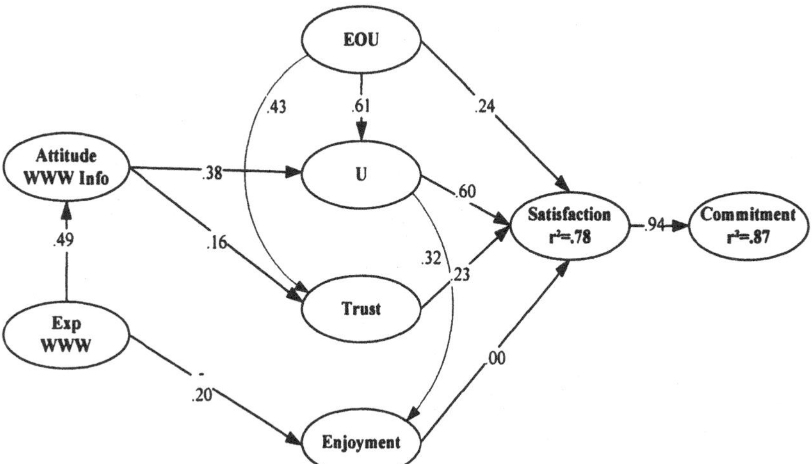

Figure 31. Alternative Structural Model with Enjoyment Instead of Exploratory Browsing Behaviour

Although the alternative model outlined in Figure 31 has quite similar influences compared to the one proposed in Figure 30, there is no influence of enjoyment on satisfaction (path insignificance at a level of $p = 0.910$). Furthermore, model fits are continuously more or less the same like for the final model ($x^2/df=3.545$, GFI=0.958, RMSEA=0.043, NFI=0.951, CFI=0.963, AGFI= 0.943). However, since enjoyment does not exert any influence on satisfaction, the model (and the hypothesis 4a that enjoyment is exerting an influence upon satisfaction) is rejected in favour of the model indicated in Figure 30.

When looking at the second alternative (excluding personal characteristics), the following model presented in Figure 32 turns out. The path coefficients are again very similar to the final model. However, fit indices are worse than for the final model, especially the RMSEA and the ratio between chi-square and the degrees of freedom which is nearly reaching the level of 5 ($x^2/df=4.815$, GFI=0.955, RMSEA=0.052, NFI=0.956, CFI=0.965, AGFI=0.939). Furthermore, the final accepted structural model includes more information by considering the antecedents (i.e. experience and attitude) of the influencing factors. Therefore, the second alternative model is not accepted as the final structural model either.

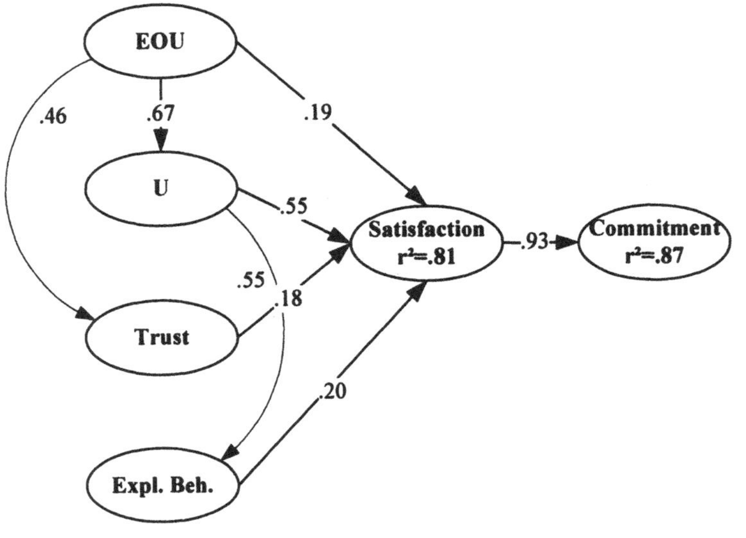

Figure 32. Alternative Structural Model without Personal Characteristics

In conclusion, the research model proposed was confirmed; some of the hypothesised relationships had to be rejected. The construct of exploratory browsing behaviour has a significant impact on satisfaction whereas enjoyment did not have in this study. Personal characteristics proved to serve as antecedents to some of the influencing factors and their inclusion in the model shows better fit indices than if they are excluded.

5.2.5 Structural Analyses for the three Personalised Internet Applications

Structural models for the respective personalised internet applications will be presented in the following sub-sections. Analyses of the three personalised internet applications were conducted with the goal to find out relevant differences in the path estimates. Such differences are likely because the web sites stem from different areas. Therefore, multiple group analysis was applied assuming that the structure of the model is the same across groups.

The focus will be on differences of path estimates only because the goal is to identify if there are differences in the influencing factors on satisfaction among the three personalised internet applications. Therefore, measurement variance will not be further outlined and factor loadings were held constant to test path estimates.

The non-invariance of the three models was tested by running a model were path estimates were first allowed to vary freely within groups. Afterwards parameter constraints were placed to be the same across groups allowing evaluating differences with the help of Chi-square difference and significance. Since experience and attitude towards online information search and e-service are neither questions targeted to the specific web site nor can they be influenced by the web site providers, they are not further considered in the multiple group analysis. Therefore, the alternative structural model outlined in Figure 32 will be used as the basis of the analyses.

When comparing the unconstrained to the constrained model a chi-square difference of 810.88 (degrees of freedom: 72) arose at a significance level of $p<0.001$, thus it is suggested that effects vary across groups. All of the estimates are significant at the level $p<0.05$. The following fit statistics are relevant to the multiple group analysis (for all of the three groups, including the constraints): $x^2 / df = 2.291$, RMSEA = 0.031, NFI = 0.931, CFI = 0.960, AIC = 1123.177. Table 37 illustrates the different path estimates for each of the personalised internet applications in the multiple group analyses.

Table 37. Path Estimates for Multiple Group Analysis (Unstandardised Estimates)

Path			Path Estimates		
			Immobilien	Learn	Tiscover
EOU	→	U	0.69	0.46	0.75
U	→	EXPLBEH	0.86	0.77	0.72
EOU	→	TRUST	0.50	0.41	0.48
EOU	→	SAT	n.s.	0.23	0.22
U	→	SAT	0.50	0.44	0.35
TRUST	→	SAT	0.21	0.11	0.12
EXPLBEH	→	SAT	0.24	0.14	0.24
SAT	→	COMMIT	1.13	0.96	1.23
R^2 (satisfaction)			0.82	0.82	0.85
R^2 (commitment)			0.86	0.86	0.91

The Critical Ratios and significance levels are displayed in Table 38. The critical ratio is the regression weight estimate divided by the standard error estimate. A critical ratio above 1.96 indicates the rejection of the null hypothesis (that there is no relationship between the two latent variables). The significance level p is another decision criterion. All of the path estimates are significant at the level of $p<0.001$ except the path of ease of use going to satisfaction for the Immobilien.net model (and the path trust to satisfaction for Tiscover).

Table 38. Multiple Group Analysis: Critical Ratios and p-level (EOU = Ease of Use, U = Usefulness. EXPLBEH = Exploratory Browsing Behaviour, SAT = Satisfaction and C.R. = Critical Ratio)

Path			Immobilien	
			C.R.	p
EOU	→	U	14.594	< 0.001
U	→	EXPLBEH	12.090	< 0.001
EOU	→	TRUST	9.914	< 0.001
EOU	→	SAT	-0.241	0.809
U	→	SAT	5.863	< 0.001
TRUST	→	SAT	5.326	< 0.001
EXPLBEH	→	SAT	5.676	< 0.001
SAT	→	COMMIT	20.402	< 0.001
Path			**Learn**	
			C.R.	**p**
EOU	→	U	11.057	< 0.001
U	→	EXPLBEH	9.958	< 0.001
EOU	→	TRUST	7.985	< 0.001
EOU	→	SAT	6.120	< 0.001
U	→	SAT	7.831	< 0.001
TRUST	→	SAT	4.583	< 0.001
EXPLBEH	→	SAT	5.240	< 0.001
SAT	→	COMMIT	19.796	< 0.001
Path			**Tiscover**	
			C.R.	**p**
EOU	→	U	11.877	< 0.001
U	→	EXPLBEH	10.668	< 0.001
EOU	→	TRUST	7.779	< 0.001
EOU	→	SAT	3.815	< 0.001
U	→	SAT	5.284	< 0.001
TRUST	→	SAT	2.768	<0.01
EXPLBEH	→	SAT	4.947	< 0.001
SAT	→	COMMIT	20.244	< 0.001

Furthermore the chi-square differences between the respective groups and the constrained and unconstrained parameters were investigated and again, the significance level p is indicated. The results are illustrated in Table 39. In the first part of the table (italicised), differences between the constrained models and the unconstrained one are presented; the other three columns contain the pair wise comparisons.

Table 39. Multiple Group Analysis – Differences in Chi-Square and Significance Level

Path			***Learn <=> Immobilien <=> Tiscover***	
			Δx^2	*p*
EOU	→	***U***	*73.493*	*<0.001*
U	→	***EXPLBEH***	*54.161*	*<0.001*
EOU	→	***TRUST***	*53.686*	*<0.001*
EOU	→	***SAT***	*66.434*	*<0.001*
U	→	***SAT***	*54.105*	*<0.001*
TRUST	→	***SAT***	*55.834*	*<0.001*
EXPLBEH	→	***SAT***	*57.612*	*<0.001*
SAT	→	***COMMIT***	69.408	<0.001
Path			***Learn <=> Immobilien***	
			Δx^2	*p*
EOU	→	**U**	46.675	0.001
U	→	**EXPLBEH**	31.673	0.002
EOU	→	**TRUST**	32.869	0.001
EOU	→	**SAT**	44.490	<0.001
U	→	**SAT**	31.572	0.002
TRUST	→	**SAT**	34.801	0.001
EXPLBEH	→	**SAT**	35.470	0.001
SAT	→	**COMMIT**	36.990	<0.001
Path			***Tiscover <=> Learn***	
			Δx^2	*p*
EOU	→	**U**	34.951	<0.001
U	→	**EXPLBEH**	20.708	n.s.

Path			Tiscover <=> Learn	
			Δx^2	*p*
EOU	→	TRUST	21.262	0.047
EOU	→	SAT	20.486	n.s.
U	→	SAT	21.308	0.046
TRUST	→	SAT	20.475	n.s.
EXPLBEH	→	SAT	23.259	0.026
SAT	→	COMMIT	34.236	0.001

Path			Tiscover <=> Immobilien	
			Δx^2	*p*
EOU	→	U	24.220	0.019
U	→	EXPLBEH	25.737	0.012
EOU	→	TRUST	23.801	0.022
EOU	→	SAT	32.550	0.001
U	→	SAT	25.819	0.011
TRUST	→	SAT	25.645	0.012
EXPLBEH	→	SAT	23.732	0.022
SAT	→	COMMIT	25.572	0.012

If all of the three groups are compared the results indicate that there are differences for all of the paths. However, if differences or similarities among groups are regarded in greater detail a few non-significant paths arise. If the groups are compared pair wise, no significant differences between the groups Tiscover and Learn for the path exploratory behaviour and usefulness, ease of use and satisfaction and finally, trust and satisfaction were found.

Although not all of the path differences of the pair wise comparisons are significant, the models resulting from multiple group analyses will be outlined in the following sub-sections to be able to capture differences. Furthermore, possible reasons for differences are given. The following figures contain unstandardised estimates because they are preferably used when comparing paths among groups because obviously variances could be different (Garson, 2006).

❖ **Structural Model for Tiscover**

Surprisingly, for Tiscover usefulness seems to play a less important role than for the other two personalised internet applications although it remains the path estimate being highest compared to the other direct influencing factors on satisfaction. The relationship between ease of use and usefulness is highest for Tiscover. Obviously, the more user-friendly the web site is perceived the higher is the perceived usefulness. The results of the pair wise comparisons of path estimates indicated in Table 39 are reflected by the structural model of Figure 33.

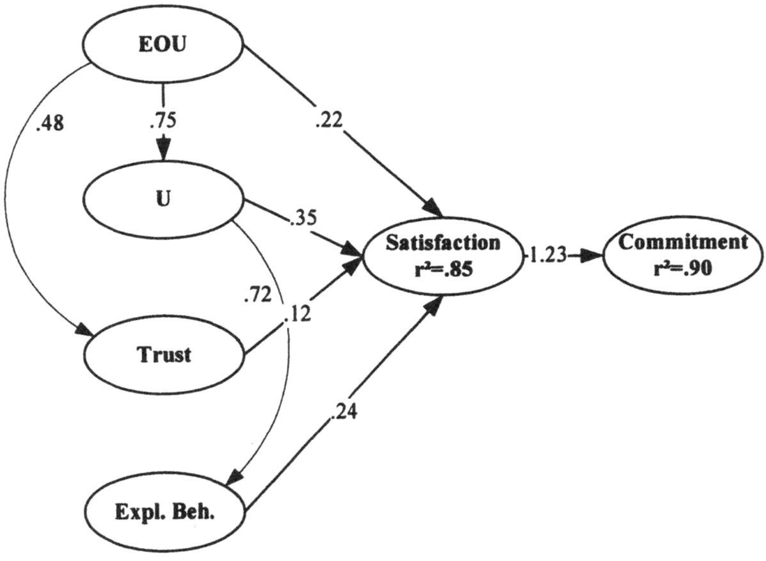

Figure 33. Partial Structural Model for Tiscover (unstandardised estimates)

The regression weights between ease of use and satisfaction is for Tiscover 0.22 and for Learn 0.23. The difference was identified as being non-significant (Table 39). The same is true for the path trust and satisfaction. The influence of trust on satisfaction is neither high for Tiscover (path estimate = 0.12) nor high for Learn@WU (path estimate = 0.11). Finally, the influence of usefulness on exploratory behaviour is high for both, Tiscover (path estimate = 0.72) and

Learn@WU (path estimate = 0.77). Again, there were no significant path differences found in the chi-square test when comparing these two personalised internet applications pair wise. Finally, the strongest model explanation is found for Tiscover, the r-square being highest for satisfaction ($R^2 = 0.85$) and commitment ($R^2 = 0.91$).

❖ Structural Model for Immobilien.net

As far as Immobilien.net is concerned (see Figure 34), ease of use does not exert a direct significant influence upon satisfaction. This might be due to the fact that ease of use was rated excellent in the case of Immobilien.net when compared to the other two systems.

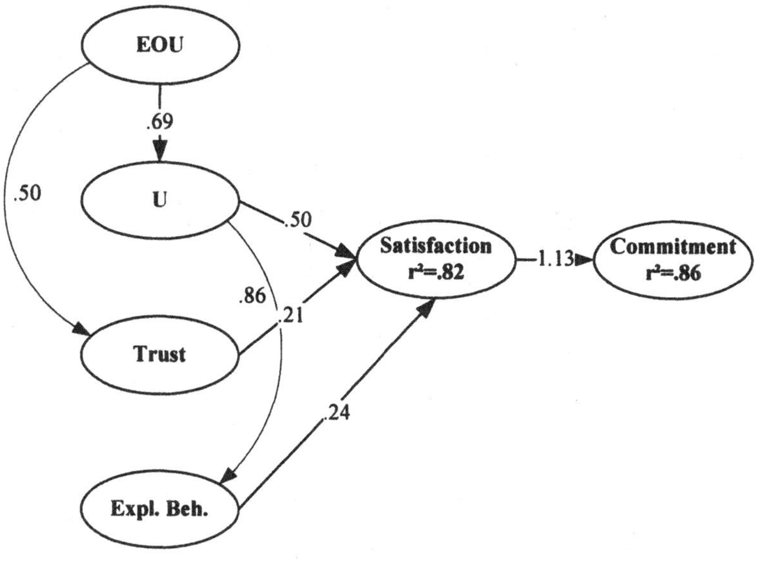

Figure 34. Partial Structural Model for Immobilien.net (unstandardised estimates)

The influence of usefulness on satisfaction was found to be highest for Immobilien.net among the three personalised internet applications. Furthermore, usefulness exerts a strong direct influence on satisfaction via exploratory browsing behaviour (path estimate = 0.86). The implication would be that the more the real estate platform is perceived to be useful, the more exploratory browsing behaviour is induced. Trust plays the highest role for satisfaction when compared to the other two systems which seems logical because real estate is usually an area in which involvement as well as perceived risk is high.

❖ **Structural Model for Learn@WU**

For the final PIA, Learn@WU, the structural model is presented in Figure 35. A lower indirect influence of ease of use on usefulness and trust was found compared to the other systems. Exploratory browsing behaviour plays a minor role which is obviously due to the fact that students want to use the web site for a goal oriented task (finding learning material, preparing an exam) rather than surfing around.

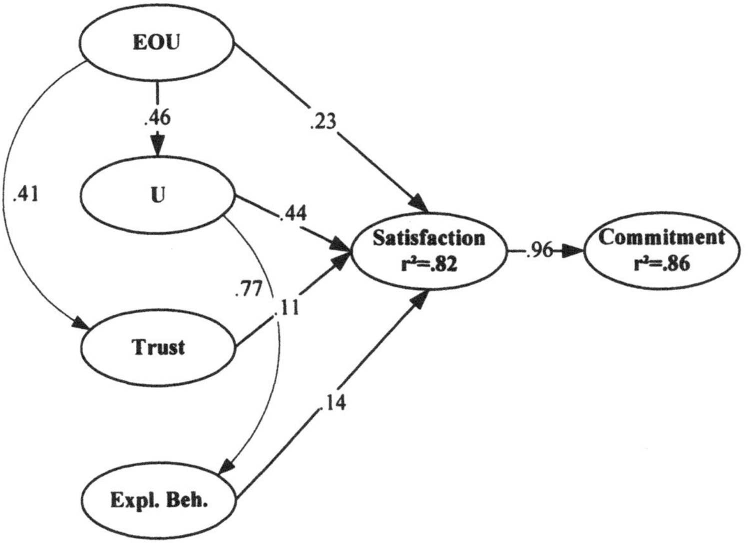

Figure 35. Partial Structural Model for Learn@WU (unstandardised estimates)

In conclusion, multiple group analyses were used to find out differences in the path estimates of the influencing factors on satisfaction. Usefulness and trust plays the highest role for Immobilien.net whereas the path of ease of use on satisfaction was not significant and very low (-0.015). Exploratory Browsing Behaviour exerts the lowest influence on satisfaction with Learn. This result reflects the differences of the systems: Immobilien.net and Tiscover both intended to induce exploratory behaviour which is not necessarily the case for Learn@WU.

A quantitative analysis was conducted to examine influencing factors on satisfaction with personalised internet applications. The research model proposed was confirmed, all of the influencing factors play a role. However, some of the relationships among the latent constructs had to be rejected. Particularly the influence of personal characteristics is not as strong as suggested.

Next, results of the expert interviews are outlined which are intended to complement the results of the user survey.

5.3 Expert Interviews

Additional to the user surveys, expert opinions were collected to get a broader point of view and to add some visionary thoughts to the results and conclusions of the study. The objective was to gain the experts' opinions on what will become important in the future. Furthermore, the experts' viewpoints about major challenges, opportunities and drawbacks of personalised systems were collected. About 25 experts (faculty members) from different disciplines (e-marketing, e-business, e-commerce, usability, psychology, computer science, design) were contacted. How were they chosen? A primary goal was to get opinions from different experts and fields as suggested by Flick (1998). Interviewees should represent a certain area and be very different from each other (List, 2005). Therefore, the goal was to get as many opinions from different fields related to the topic of personalised internet applications. Finally, eleven of the experts contacted agreed to participate in an expert interview. The questions were targeted to personalised web sites and comprised the constructs used for the survey.

During a stay as a visiting researcher at the University of Sunderland, UK, these 11 expert interviews were conducted throughout the U.K. The experts came from fields such as e-business, e-marketing, usability or computer science. The interviews were structured according to the constructs of the user survey: ease of use, usefulness, trust and exploratory behaviour. The interviews consisted of a short explanation of each construct to ensure that the interviewer and the interviewee talk about the same topic. The last question focused on additional factors that play a role either already now or in the future. Moreover, trust was further outlined by asking "Do you think people realise or take attention to if they deal with an https site?" and "Do you think that people avoid buying something via the Internet because of security concerns?" The interview guide is included in the appendix. The statements presented in the following are entirely based on the experts' comments.

This section consists of a general discussion of the method of expert or in-depth interviews. Then, the results of the expert interviews are presented.

5.3.1 Method of Expert Interviews

In-depth personal interview was the data collection method applied. The qualitative method of in-depth interviewing (also known as unstructured or semi-structured and informal interview) is an appropriate technique to gain respondents' point of views, ideas, perspectives or experiences (Berry, 1995; List, 2005). Important characteristics are that in-depth interviews follow a rather flexible approach by asking open questions and encouraging respondents to elaborate rather than restricting the interviewees (Botha, 2001).

For this study a semi-structured interview guide with open questions was employed. The interviews were intended to last for about 45 minutes. However, in most cases, interviews were resulting in interesting discussions being longer than those 45 minutes scheduled.

According to Dey (1993) a qualitative analysis is a process consisting of three steps: describing, connecting and classifying. Therefore, in the present analysis issues are classified according to the same categories like in the user survey. Soon after each interview a summary was written. The next step was to structure the statements according to pre-determined categories applied already in the user survey. Afterwards, statements were categorised in certain sub-topics.

The data collected by the expert interviews is summarised by content analysis. Content analysis can be defined as a systematic approach to receive replicable and valid inferences from text (Krippendorff, 2004; Weber, 1990). A lot of words and text can be compressed and classified into fewer content categories (Weber, 1990). Content analysis is a research tool used to gain new insights or knowledge about particular phenomena by making inferences from texts (Krippendorff, 2004). The method of content analysis can be described as summarising content of data by counting aspects arising in any form (such as group discussions, text or interviews) of content (List, 2005). The advantage of simplifying statements, summarising and counting them is to decrease subjectivity (List, 2005).

5.3.2 Results of Expert Interviews

The following paragraphs intend to give an overview of the topics mentioned by the experts. They are categorised according to the dimensions applied in the user survey. Each dimension includes several sub-topics introduced by the experts and analysed according to their content. For the sake of better understandability not only single words but also some statements are indicated. They are presented in tables ranked according to their frequency of occurrence. If issues are mentioned just by one expert, they are described in the text; otherwise they are highlighted in the tables.

5.3.2.1 Ease of Use

When thinking of ease of use, experts argued that the structure and hierarchy of information is important. The comparison with a TV or DVD manual was mentioned: first there should be a certain level of basic information and only if needed the user can explore more of the content. The load of information is another crucial issue, it is recommended to use not more than 6 or 7 headings on one site. However, two experts suggested that one should refrain from such general guidelines such as three columns is the accepted format and is the customer's expectation. The type of font is important as well. Sans-serif types such as Verdana are definitely better than e.g. Times New Roman. Download time for files is another crucial issue and should be kept as short as possible.

The difficulty to match users' and designers' expectations at the same time was mentioned. Moreover, the marketing department should be involved as well when deciding about the web site's content and structure (creating a web site is not just a technical issue). Ease of use should also be adjusted to the target market and also to different groups of people including disabled such as colour-blind, not so experienced ones or elderly people. Furthermore, cultural differences do play a role e.g. in navigation. When it comes to different browsers (like Mozilla Firefox versus Internet Explorer) or different computer systems (like Mac), the web sites should be displayed in all of the systems without problems. Plug-ins should be avoided. In general, a rather older version of programs should be used so that everybody can access the web site easily. The lowest common denominator should be chosen. There are still too many technical messages (e.g. error number 404) and technology should not be used just for technology's sake. One expert suggested that if the web site includes search facilities it could mean that the site's navigation is not good.

When it comes to the visual appearance, the experts mentioned that there should not be too many pictures included in the web site because download time could be increased significantly. Loading time should definitely be considered. Bandwidth was mentioned several times. According to the experts the speed of bandwidth is still an important factor. Studies have shown that after approximately seven seconds users switch to another site although perceptions towards loading time vary across countries, e.g. in the U.K. Three seconds of loading time are usually accepted whereas in China users are prepared to wait for eight seconds. Therefore, the loading time has to be considered, there is still not everybody equipped with broadband connection. A simple web site with fewer pictures, less information is best because users want to scan a web site quickly.

One expert suggested that every page should have the same design because it is possible that the users don't go directly to the home page but enter another page. Furthermore, white space was named which should be included to divide different sections of the web sites. In general, the middle of the web site is most important. There have to be some key points in the web site structure that users can easily scan the web site. Navigation is a crucial issue. However, help functions should be provided. Web sites must be differently structured than tangible, printed media. As far as input forms are concerned it has to be clearly stated what is needed when filling in forms. Users are annoyed when they have to go back (because they have forgotten to fill in something) and all previous inputs are lost.

Another crucial point is to which domain the web sites belong. For some web sites e.g. an online grocery store a certain level of ease of use might be enough. Amazon was named as an example of not being really usable despite its success.

In conclusion, two experts mentioned that one should refrain from sticking to standard guidelines too much. All of the issues which were mentioned more than once (and were described above) are outlined in Table 40.

Table 40. Ease of Use Issues Named by Experts

Ease of Use Issues	Absolute Number of Counts
Ease of use issue depends strongly upon target audience (age, culture, disabilities, familiarity)	7
Bandwidth and loading time are important	6
Structure, hierarchy is important	3
Reliability – is the web site often crashing?	3
Load of information is crucial	2
Difficulty to match users' and designers' expectations	2
Refrain from using standard guidelines	2
Simplicity of the web site	2

5.3.2.2 Usefulness

First, one expert suggested that knowledge about the target market is important to determine which content should be displayed. Objectives are vital; customer expectations do play a significant role. Two different web site versions could make sense, e.g. in the travel industry: one for business and one for leisure travellers (because they usually have different information needs). Furthermore, the place where people are surfing could be taken into account as well, are they browsing the web site at home where they might have more time but lower bandwidth or are they using the web site in the office where the opposite is likely to be the case? This issue was named by another expert as well but in the context of mobile devices. A text only version for mobile devices should be provided. Furthermore, a web site should help to buy, to make decisions and to provide the information which is needed. A 24 hours availability and instant reply are additional crucial issues expected by customers.

Table 41. Usefulness Issues Named by Experts

Usefulness Issues	Absolute Number of Counts
Accuracy: information which is up to date	3
Different version of a web site: business & leisure, mobile	2
Goal of the web site visit (goal directed vs. hedonic motivations) is important	2

Table 41 outlines that accuracy was perceived as very important by the experts. They also emphasised that content could be structured according to the context in which it is used e.g. business versus leisure travel content.

When they were asked to prioritise between usefulness and ease of use, two of the experts suggested usefulness to be more important and another two experts favoured ease of use being more crucial than usefulness, the others thinking both are equally important or it depends upon the web site context. It was argued that perceived ease of use influences perceived usefulness. Furthermore, both factors depend strongly on the situation and motivation to visit the web site. The objective is crucial: is the visit just about surfing around or is it rather a goal-oriented visit? The user might tolerate shortcomings easier if they have no alternative or not a lot of choice for a certain type of web site.

5.3.2.3 Trust

Three of the experts stated that paying via the WWW is as risky as giving away your credit card in a restaurant (see Table 42). If a third party is doing the payment procedure it is also problematic because then the user is taken to another site. A lot of people know about the importance of secure connections and transactions. However, it depends upon the whole web site, the site design rather than on technical aspects. Is the site as a whole trustworthy, for instance a logo might be helpful. A brand or trademark plays a role – is the web site provider a small company or a reputable one? Is it a newly established company or a well-known one? Trust is more about the perception than about the reality. Perceived trust strongly depends upon the circumstances, the nature of activities, the perception a user gets from the web site. Furthermore, a statement which technology is used and how privacy is protected and security is ensured could be useful. An imprint (containing information about the organisation, their address and goals pursued with the web site presence) and contact numbers or call back service could help to build up trust and credibility. Phone or fax numbers should be indicated to make complaints or feedback possible via traditional channels as well.

Trust statements or certificates should be placed very prominently because users usually have a natural distrust and there is still some reluctance to buy via the WWW because of trust issues.

Trust issues do play a particular role for new web sites, it is not only about payment and personal data but also the objectiveness of the content is crucial. Furthermore, commitment and honesty are important. When thinking of trust the whole experience could be included (also the service before and after an online purchase). The level of caution depends also upon the type of web site. However, in general, people are quite cautious and do not store credit card details. The crucial question is: who is listening in (and not who is the vendor)?

Trust is extremely important concerning bookings and e-commerce. Several experts agreed that fraud and crimes committed via the Internet will even rise in the future. Even if people have trust in a company they do not automatically trust the payment procedure. The focus will be set more and more on certificates. For small companies it will be easier to have a contract with secure transaction businesses. Web site owners not providing secure connections will soon have the reputation of being unprofessional.

Furthermore, four experts were convinced people do not yet pay attention to encrypted web sites (e.g. https). However, two suggested that the majority of people do so. The majority of the experts agreed upon the statement that people avoid buying via the Internet because of security concerns. However, it was suggested that it depends strongly upon the type of products or services purchased, e.g. in the case of books and CDs it is quite common and convenient to buy via the WWW whereas it is less common to buy clothes. One expert suggested that the importance of trust and security is far too much exaggerated and two of the experts emphasised that the online world is as secure as the offline one.

Table 42. Trust Issues Named by Experts

Trust Issues	Absolute Number of Counts
People still avoid buying via the Internet because of trust concerns	9
Is it a reputable web site/company or a small, newly established?	5
Conventional ways (e.g. the phone) are used instead of the WWW to purchase although the information is obtained via the WWW	4
More risky to give away credit card in restaurants	3
Privacy, security policy or liability statement could help to increase trust	3
Phishing, fake web sites make users worrying	2
The whole impression of the web site is important	2
Trust plays a higher role for older people	2
Trust is the most important influencing factor	2
The WWW is as secure as the offline world	2

In conclusion, trust and security concerns were a major issue for most of the experts which can also be noted by the amount of topics mentioned by them. An increasing number of fraud incidents will make these concerns even more significant in the future.

5.3.2.4 Exploratory Browsing Behaviour

Pleasing experiences are necessary for some domains in the offline as well as in the online environment. Especially the retail online environment is predestined to create an inviting, encouraging atmosphere. Furthermore, the longer a user stays the more he or she probably buys. The entertainment factor, hedonic and experiential aspects are clearly underutilised at the moment. "Funology", "Enjoyability" may override other influencing factors according to one expert's opinion. However, one limitation is that the online environment cannot appeal to all of the human senses, e.g. smelling.

One expert suggested that aesthetics play without a doubt a significant role for web site satisfaction. Another stated that the goal pursued with the web site visit is crucial to assess if exploratory browsing behaviour is important to satisfaction. For web sites predominantly used in leisure, exploratory browsing behaviour could be an influencing factor whereas for work related web sites it is less likely. Furthermore, whether exploratory browsing behaviour is important or not depends on the audience and the attitude of the users. Fun is not an essential factor if it detracts from usefulness it is rather a hindrance. One expert guessed that for 80% of the web sites exploratory browsing does not have any influence.

Furthermore, time might be the more important issue which prevents users from exploring the web site. On the other hand, an important factor is that the web site is able to draw and hold a user's attention, spark interest and make inquisitive. One expert suggested that the issue of fun and exploratory behaviour depends upon demographics and age. It is important for younger users but less important for older people.

In conclusion, the majority of the experts thought that fun, excitement, exploratory browsing, experiential aspects could be an additional factor but does not have top priority. The whole purpose or message of the web site should not be forgotten and fun aspects should not be exaggerated when designing the web site. Two of the experts even thought that fun could be irritating or constitute a hindrance to use the web site properly. According to one expert a web site has to be as simple as possible and fun does not produce any value-added. However, there might be contexts in which fun or exploratory browsing behaviour play a role, e.g. in travel.

Table 43. Opinions on Exploratory Browsing Behaviour

Exploratory Browsing Issues	Absolute Number of Counts
Aesthetics, pleasing experiences are important	3
Goal is crucial	2
Time is usually more important	2
Type of web site (e.g. for leisure web sites more important)	2
Demography-dependent	2
Fun attracting parts of a web site could be a hindrance or irritating	2

5.3.2.5 Additional Crucial Factors and Outlook

Finally, experts were asked if they think there are other crucial issues previously not mentioned and issues they think would become important in the future. As far as the Uniform Resource Identifier (URI) or domain names are considered it is not too important for Europe but in the U.S. users do look at domain names, according to one of the expert's assessment. Another expert stated that the URI name is a major issue also contributing to credibility (see Table 44). Furthermore, the web site should seem professional; a personal touch is very dangerous, though it depends upon the culture of the company. The web site could be light-hearted, informal if the company is as well. However, it should not be jokey or funny. The competition is just only one click away, so everything that could upset customers should be avoided. Pop-ups are a good example; they are usually annoying the customer rather than helping.

The web site should fit into the e-business strategy and is not just a marketing tool any more nor is it a technical issue. Furthermore, what drives satisfaction is different among different domains and the perception of satisfaction and its influencing factors changes very fast.

There should be a certain level of value for both the user and the company. For the customers the most common value is the usefulness of the web site. For the company the main value would be to sell something, to provide a confident picture of the company or the diffusion of good image. For companies it could be important to explore niche markets.

The empowerment of users is important; they want to be in control of what they are doing. Furthermore, word of mouth could be crucial meaning users are recommending the web site to others. Virtual communities like Google or Yahoo were predicted to increase in importance in the future. Personal contact possibilities were mentioned and the possibility to give feedback. Links to other web sites could make sense. Finally, a competitive advantage could be to present novel information, products or services.

Table 44. Further Crucial Issues

Other Issues	Absolute Number of Counts
Personalisation should be possible (but should not be a must)	3
Domain name is important	2
Visuals, graphics, colours	2
Sophistication/Professionalism, the web site has to have a good quality, e.g. maps	2

In conclusion, opinions on the most important influencing factors on satisfaction with personalised internet applications were different. However, exploratory browsing or fun aspects were prioritised by only one expert. Usefulness and trust were both explicitly named as being most important by two experts. Ease of use was not explicitly mentioned as being the most important factor. However, the number of comments on ease of use suggests a high level of significance.

6 DISCUSSION AND OUTLOOK

6.1 Conclusion

The conclusion will briefly summarise the core constructs of the research model and the outcome of the analyses. Furthermore, the importance of this study will be outlined and which implications are expected.

There is a vast amount of information on the Internet and it becomes more and more important to offer convenient tools for the user to filter out relevant information. Recommender and personalised systems offer the possibility to propose the user targeted and tailored results. These types of web sites are more complex than usual ones and therefore need thorough investigation.

The study aimed to test a comprehensive explanatory model for system satisfaction including several system and personal factors. A research model and its dimensions were proposed on the basis of existing studies. The measurement scale was developed by using items applied in previous studies or by suggesting own questions and pre-testing them. Finally, a user evaluation of three personalised internet applications was conducted and the online user survey resulted in a sample size of 1386. Structural Equation Modelling was used to identify important influencing factors on system satisfaction with three personalised internet applications. However, the scope of the findings can be much broader and of general significance for PIAs, since the ones used for the evaluation stem from three different areas.

First, the construct of usefulness is a necessary characteristic and was found to have the highest influence on satisfaction with a personalised internet application. A system can be very easy to use but if the information contained is not relevant or up-to-date it is useless. On the other hand, ease of use or system quality does play an important role as well. If information is not found, it is once again useless. Trust is a significant construct because of the increasing sales function of the Internet but also if the focus is on a high risk product or service like real estates. Hedonic benefits, like exploratory browsing behaviour (EBB) can play a role as well although the influence varies across systems. The influence of EBB for the e-learning platform was rather low compared to the travel web site and the real estate platform. This assumption seems logical: EBB does not play a role for personalised internet applications predominantly used for goal-directed behaviour. Finally, personal characteristics such as experience and attitude towards the Internet have an influence when interacting with a website. However, the effect hypothesised was stronger than it turned out to be when tested with empirical data. Internet familiarity served only as antecedent of attitude towards information search via the WWW and had a negative impact upon EBB. The assumptions that internet familiarity also exerts a direct influence upon satisfaction and an indirect via trust, usefulness and ease of use were not confirmed. Attitude showed no direct influence on satisfaction either but indirect effects were found via usefulness and trust.

The method of expert interviews was used to complement the results of structural equation modelling. Furthermore, opinions about future developments, challenges, risks and opportunities were captured by the expert interviews which would not have been possible to gain by the user survey. The majority of the experts considered ease of use still as one of the major influencing factors when looking at the number of issues named. However, they argued that trust will become increasingly important in the future because more and more cases and types of internet fraud arose. Moreover, issues like domain names, personalisation, visual appeal and sophistication when designing the web site were mentioned.

6.2 Implications for Practitioners

What are the implications for providers of personalised internet applications? Results can provide proposals to design recommender and personalised systems more satisfactorily for the user. Structural Equation Modelling showed that usefulness is still the dominant factor positively influencing satisfaction with personalised internet applications. Therefore, the content of the personalised internet applications should be kept as accurate and helpful as possible no matter in which domain the provider is operating.

Exploratory browsing should be facilitated depending on the web site. As shown in the multiple group analysis it does play a more important role for the real estate web site and the travel platform which both offer a lot of information additional to the search of real estate or travel products and services. However, in the case of Learn@WU its effect was rather negligible.

Trust had a higher influence on satisfaction with the real estate platform compared to the other two systems. Thus, for high risky products or services like real estate are, special attention should be paid to trust building cues like certificates or security and privacy statements (as mentioned by the experts).

Attitude towards information search via the WWW and the use of e-service and Internet familiarity serve as antecedents for usefulness, trust and exploratory behaviour. Personal characteristics did not have a direct influence on satisfaction. This could be a good result for the providers of personalised internet applications because they cannot or can only hardly influence personal characteristics (e.g. expectations could be influenced to a certain degree).

In conclusion, ease of use and usefulness do play a role for most (if not all) web sites or personalised internet applications. The effect of trust towards the web site and how information is processed strongly depends on the type of web site. The same is true for exploratory browsing behaviour.

6.3 Limitations and Implications for Future Research

One of the obvious shortcomings is that the sample consists of rather experienced users. Furthermore, the number of study participants already knowing the web sites was rather high considering the way how people were invited to answer the questionnaires. Newsletters and postings at the respective web sites were primarily used to encourage people to participate in the user survey. Therefore, the inclusion of a higher number of study participants who are not particularly familiar with the Internet and who don't have knowledge of the respective web sites could be fruitful and offer new insights.

Future studies could concentrate more specifically on recommender systems which was not the case in this study. The availability of recommenders (particularly German systems) was not given and therefore, the requirements were lowered and the study focused on personalised internet applications. However, recommender systems are often handled as the type of systems having most potential to create a satisfactory online user experience. Therefore, further research on the influencing factors on satisfaction with online recommender systems should be conducted.

As far as the research model is concerned, further research from the methodological point of view could involve Inferred Causation Theory (ICT).

Directions of causality could be checked as proposed by Pearl (2001). Moreover, latent class analysis could be applied with the goal to either confirm the grouping because of the different samples (different web sites) or if grouping based on other personal characteristics of the sample such as attitude or experience is more appropriate.

In future studies the type of internet application could be considered more explicitly and different types could be compared to each other in terms of usefulness or hedonic aspects. Is it a web site which is rather used for goal directed behaviour or which should also provide some kind of fun? The influence of exploratory browsing behaviour or trust is likely to vary across systems.

What is the most appropriate construct to measure hedonic related aspects or intrinsically motivated user behaviour? Further research could focus on the constructs of Exploratory Browsing versus enjoyment, playfulness or Flow because their influence could become even stronger in the future.

References

Aamodt, A. & E. Plaza (1994). Case-Based Reasoning: Foundational Issues, Methodological Variations, and System Approaches. AICom - Artificial Intelligence Communications, 7(1), 39-59.

Adomavicius, G. & A. Tuzhilin (2002). An Architecture of E-Butler: A Consumer-Centric Online Personalization System. International Journal of Computational Intelligence & Application, 2(3), 313-328.

Adomavicius, G. & A. Tuzhilin (2005a). Personalization Technologies: A Process-Oriented Perspective. Communications of the ACM, 48 (10), 83-92.

Adomavicius, G. & A. Tuzhilin (2005b). Toward the Next Generation of Recommender Systems: A Survey of State-of-the-Art and Possible Extensions. IEEE Transactions on Knowledge and Data Engineering, 17(2), 734-749.

Agarwal, R. & E. Karahanna (2000). Time Flies When You're Having Fun: Cognitive Absorption and Beliefs About Information Technology Usage. MIS Quarterly, 24(4), 665-695.

Ajzen, I. (1991). The Theory of Planned Behavior. Organizational Behavior and Human Decision Processes, 50, 179-211.

Albers, S. & L. Hildebrandt (2006). Methodische Probleme bei der Erfolgsfaktorenforschung - Messfehler, Formative Versus Reflektive Indikatoren und die Wahl des Strukturgleichungs-Modells. Zeitschrift für betriebswirtschaftliche Forschung, February, 2-33.

Anderson, B. (2003). The Domestication of Information and Communication Technologies, (University of Essex, Working Paper).

Anderson, J. C. & D. W. Gerbing (1988). Structural Equation Modeling in Practice: A Review and Recommended Two-Step Approach. Psychological Bulletin, 103(3), 411-423.

Anderson, R. E. & S. S. Srinivasan (2003). E-Satisfaction and E-Loyalty: A Contingency Framework. Psychology & Marketing, 20(2), 123-138.

Ansari, A., S. Essegaier & R. Kohli (2000). Internet Recommendation Systems. Journal of Marketing Research, 37, 363-375.

Ansari, A. & C. F. Mela (2003). E-Customization. Journal of Marketing Research, 40(2), 131-145.

Arnold, M. J. & K. E. Reynolds (2003). Hedonic Shopping Motivations. Journal of Retailing, 79(2), 77-95.

Ba, S. & P. A. Pavlou (2002). Evidence of the Effect of Trust Building Technology in Electronic Markets: Price Premiums and Buyer Behavior. MIS Quarterly, 26(3), 243-268.

Backhaus, K., B. Erichson, W. Plinke & R. Weiber (1994). Multivariate Analysemethoden. Berlin, Heidelberg: Springer.

Backhaus, K., B. Erichson, W. Plinke & R. Weiber (2003). Strukturgleichungsmodelle. In: Multivariate Analysemethoden: Eine anwendungsorientierte Einführung. pp. 333-415. Berlin: Springer.

Bagozzi, R. P. & Y. Yi (1988). On the Evaluation of Structural Equation Models. Journal of the Academy of Marketing Science, 16, 74-94.

Barnes, S. I. & R. Vidgen (2001). An Evaluation of Cyber-Bookshops: The Webqual Method. International Journal of Electronic Commerce, 6(1), 11-31.

Barnes, S. J. & R. Vidgen (2003). Measuring Web Site Quality Improvements: A Case Study of the Forum on Strategic Management Knowledge Exchange. Industrial Management and Data Systems, 103(5/6), 297-310.

Bauernfeind, U. & A. Zins (2006). The Perception of Exploratory Browsing and Trust with Recommender Websites. Journal of Information Technology and Tourism, 8(2), 121-136.

Baumgartner, H. & C. Homburg (1996). Applications of Structural Equation Modeling in Marketing and Consumer Research: A Review. International Journal of Research in Marketing, 13(2), 139-161.

Baumgartner, H. & J.-B. Steenkamp (1996). Exploratory Consumer Buying Behavior: Conceptualization and Measurement. International Journal of Research in Marketing, 13(2), 121-137.

Benbunan-Fich, R. (2001). Using Protocol Analysis to Evaluate the Usability of a Commercial Web Site. Information & Management, 39(2), 151-163.

Berger, H., M. Dittenbach & D. Merkl (2004). User-Oriented Evaluation of a Natural Language Tourism Information System. Information Technology & Tourism, 6(3), 167- 180.

Berry, R. S. (1995). Collecting Data by In-Depth Interviewing. In: British Educational Research Association Annual Conference, Brighton, UK.

Bettman, J. R. & M. F. Luce (1998). Constructive Consumer Choice Processes. Journal of Consumer Research, 25(3), 187-218.

Betts, M. (2001). Turning Browsers into Buyers. MIT Sloan Management Review, 42(2), 8-9.

Bhattacherjee, A. (2001). Understanding Information Systems Continuance: An Expectation-Confirmation Model. MIS Quarterly, 25(3), 351-370.

Bhattacherjee, A. & G. Premkumar (2004). Understanding Changes in Belief and Attitude toward Information Technology Usage: A Theoretical Model and Longitudinal Test. MIS Quarterly, 28(2), 229-254.

Bitner, M. J. (1992). Servicescapes: The Impact of Physical Surroundings on Customers and Employees. Journal of Marketing, 56(2), 57-72.

Blackmon, M. H., P. G. Polson, M. Kitajima & C. Lewis (2002). Cognitive Walkthrough for the Web. In: ACM Conference on Human Factors in Computing Systems (CHI'2002), 463-470.

Blili, S., L. Raymond & S. Rivard (1998). Impact of Task Uncertainty, End-User Involvement, and Competence on the Success of End-User Computing. Information & Management, 33(3), 137-153.

Blom, J. (2000). Personalization - a Taxonomy. In: Conference on Human Factors in Computing Systems (CHI' 00), The Hague, Netherlands.

Blom, J. (2002). A Theory of Personalized Recommendations. In: Conference on Human Factors in Computing Systems (CHI' 02), Minneapolis, USA.

Bollen, K. A. (1989). Structural Equations with Latent Variables. New York: Wiley.

Botha, P. P. (2001). The Qualitative Interview as Data-Gathering Technique: Strengths and Weaknesses. Journal of Family Ecology and Consumer Sciences, 29, 13-19.

Brooke, J. (1986). SUS - a Quick and Dirty Usability Scale. http://www.cee.hw.ac.uk/~ph/sus.html.

Byrne, B. M. (2001). Structural Equation Modeling with Amos. Mahwah, NJ: Erlbaum.

Cantoni, V., M. Cellario & M. Porta (2004). Perspectives and Challenges in E-Learning: Towards Natural Interaction Paradigms. Journal of Visual Languages & Computing, 15(5), 333-345.

Carmel, E., R. D. Whitaker & J. F. George (1993). PD and Joint Application Design: A Transatlantic Comparison. Association for Computing Machinery. Communications of the ACM, 36(6), 40-49.

Carton, L. (2002). Emarket News: Only 26% of Users Trust E-Commerce Web Sites. How to Establish Trust on a Site? http://www.emarketnews.com/archives/2002-5/ecommerceprint.htm.

Chan, S.-C. & M. Lu (2004). Understanding Internet Banking Adoption and Use Behavior: A Hong Kong Perspective. Journal of Global Information Management, 12(3), 21-44.

Chen, C.-M., H.-M. Lee & Y.-H. Chen (2004). Personalized E-Learning System Using Item Response Theory. Computers & Education, 44(3), 237-255.

Chen, L.-D. & J. Tan (2004). Technology Adaptation in E-Commerce: Key Determinants of Virtual Stores Acceptance. European Management Journal, 22(1), 74-86.

Cheung, W., M. K. Chang & V. S. Lai (2000). Prediction of Internet and World Wide Web Usage at Work: A Test of an Extended Triandis Model. Decision Support Systems, 30(1), 83-100.

Childers, T. L., C. L. Carr, J. Peck & S. Carson (2001). Hedonic and Utilitarian Motivations for Online Retail Shopping Behavior. Journal of Retailing, 77(4), 511-535.

Chin, J. P., V. A. Diehl & K. L. Norman (1988). Questionnaire for User Interaction Satisfaction (QUIS). In: Proceedings of of the ACM SIGCHI '88 Conference on Human Factors in Computing Systems, Washington (DC), USA.

Chin, W. W. (1998). Issues and Opinion on Structural Equation Modeling. MIS Quarterly, 22(1), 12-22.

Chiou, J.-S. (2004). The Antecedents of Consumers' Loyalty toward Internet Service Providers. Information & Management, 41(6), 685-695.

Cho, Y. H., J. K. Kim & S. H. Kim (2002). A Personalized Recommender System Based on Web Usage Mining and Decision Tree Induction. Expert Systems with Applications, 23(3), 329-342.

Chung, J. & F. B. Tan (2004). Antecedents of Perceived Playfulness: An Exploratory Study on User Acceptance of General Information-Searching Websites. Information & Management, 41(7), 869-881.

Cingil, I., A. Dogac & A. Azgin (2000). A Broader Approach to Personalization. Association for Computing Machinery. Communications of the ACM, 43(8), 136-141.

Cooley, R., B. Mobasher & J. Srivastava (1997). Web Mining: Information and Pattern Discovery on the World Wide Web. In: 9th IEEE International Conference on Tools with Artificial Intelligence (ICTAI'97), 558-567.

Csikszentmihalyi, M. (1975). Beyond Boredom and Anxiety. San Francisco, California: Jossey-Bass.

Davidson, E. J. (1999). Joint Application Design (JAD) in Practice. Journal of Systems and Software, 45(3), 215-223.

Davis, F., R. Bagozzi & P. Warsaw (1992). Extrinsic and Intrinsic Motivation to Use Computers in Workplace. Journal of Applied Social Psychology, 22, 1111-1132.

Davis, F. D. (1989). Perceived Usefulness, Perceived Ease of Use, and User Acceptance of Information Technology. MIS Quarterly, 38(3), 319-339.

Davis, F. D., R. P. Bagozzi & P. R. Warshaw (1989). User Acceptance of Computer Technology: A Comparison of Two Theoretical Models. Management Science, 35(8), 982-1003.

DeLone, W. H. & E. R. Mc Lean (2002). Information Systems Success Revisited. In: Proceedings of the 35th Hawaii International Conference on System Sciences, 238-249. Big Island, Hawaii: IEEE.

DeLone, W. H. & E. R. McLean (1992). Information Systems Success: The Quest for the Dependent Variable. Information Systems Research, 3(1), 60-95.

DeLone, W. H. & E. R. McLean (2003). The Delone and Mclean Model of Information Systems Success: A Ten-Year Update. Journal of Management Information Systems, 19(4), 9-30.

Dey, I. (1993). Qualitative Data Analysis. A User-Friendly Guide for Social Scientists. London, New York: Routledge.

Diamantopoulos, A. & B. Schlegelmilch (1997). Taking the Fear out of Data Analysis. A Step-by-Step Approach. London: The Dryden Press.

Diamantopoulos, A. & H. M. Winklhofer (2001). Index Construction with Formative Indicators: An Alternative to Scale Development. Journal of Marketing Research, 38(2), 269-277.

Dillon, R. R. (2003). Usability Testing: Myths, Misconceptions and Misuses. http://www.carleton.ca/hotlab/hottopics/Articles/usability_myths.html.

Doll, W. J. & G. Torkzadeh (1988). The Measurement of End-User Computing Satisfaction. MIS Quarterly, 12(2), 259-274.

Dos Santos, B. L. & M. L. Bariff (1988). A Study of User Interface Aids for Model-Oriented Decision Support Systems. Management Science, 34(4), 461-468.

Dos Santos, B. L. & K. Peffers (1998). Competitor and Vendor Influence on the Adoption of Innovative Applications in Electronic Commerce. Information & Management, 34(3), 175-184.

Duncan, O. D. (1975). Introduction to Structural Equation Models. New York: Academic Press.

Eggert, A. & G. Fassott (2003). Zur Verwendung Formativer und Reflektiver Indikatoren in Strukturgleichungsmodellen. Kaiserslauter Schriftenreihe Marketing, Issue 20.

Eighmey, J. & L. McCord (1998). Adding Value in the Information Age: Uses and Gratifications of Sites on the World Wide Web. Journal of Business Research, 41(3), 187-194.

eMarketer (2005). Western Europe E-Commerce: Spotlight on the UK, Germany and France. http://www.mindbranch.com/catalog/product.jsp?code=R203-345.

Eroglu, S. A., K. A. Machleit & L. M. Davis (2003). Empirical Testing of a Model of Online Store Atmospherics and Shopper Responses. Psychology & Marketing, 20(2), 139-152.

Finneran, C. M. & P. Zhang (2003). A Person-Artefact-Task (PAT) Model of Flow Antecedents in Computer-Mediated Environments. International Journal of Human-Computer Studies, 59(4), 475-496.

Fishbein, M. & I. Ajzen (1975). Belief, Attitude, Intention, and Behavior: An Introduction to Theory and Research. Reading, MA: Addison-Wesley.

Fornell, C. & D. F. Larcker (1981). Evaluating Structural Equation Models with Unobservable Variables and Measurement Error. Journal of Marketing Research, 18(1), 39-50.

Galan, J.-P. & C. Gonzalez (2001). Webscape: A Theoretical Framework of Web Site Design Impact on Consumers' Responses. European Advances in Consumer Research, 5, 270-275.

Garson, D. (2006). Structural Equation Modeling. http://www2.chass.ncsu.edu/garson/pa765/structur.htm.

Gasson, S. (2003). Human-Centered Vs. User-Centered Approaches to Information System Design. JITTA : Journal of Information Technology Theory and Application, 5(2), 29-46.

Gefen, D. (2000). E-Commerce: The Role of Familiarity and Trust. Omega, 28(6), 725-737.

Gefen, D. & D. W. Straub (2004). Consumer Trust in B2c E-Commerce and the Importance of Social Presence: Experiments in E-Products and E-Services. Omega, 32(6), 407-424.

Goldsmith, R. E. (2002). Explaining and Predicting the Consumer Intention to Purchase over the Internet: An Exploratory Study. Journal of Marketing Theory & Practice, 10(2), 22-30.

Gonzáles, G., B. López & J. L. de la Rosa (2002). The Emotional Factor: An Innovative Approach to User Modelling for Recommender Systems. In: Workshop on Recommendation and Personalization in eCommerce, Malaga, Spain.

Greer, T. H. & M. B. Murtaza (2003). Web Personalization: The Impact of Perceived Innovation Characteristics on the Intention to Use Personalization. The Journal of Computer Information Systems, 43(3), 50-54.

Groß, T. & A.-R. Sadeghi (2001). Empfehlungssysteme. Seminar: Quality of Service in E-Commerce. Saarland University.

Human Factors Research Group (2002). Software Usability Measurement Inventory (SUMI). http://www.ucc.ie/hfrg/questionnaires/sumi/index.html.

Guion, L. A. (2006). Conducting an In-Depth Interview. http://edis.ifas.ufl.edu/FY393.

Ha, S. H. (2002). Helping Online Customers Decide through Web Personalization. IEEE Intelligent Systems, 17(6), 34-43.

Habib, L. (2003). Domestication of E-Learning Technologies: A Preliminary Conceptual Framework. In: NOKOBIT 2003, Oslo, Norway.

Habib, L. & T. Cornford (2001). Computers in the Home: Domestic Technology and the Process of Domestication. In: European Conference on Information Systems, Bled, Slovenia.

Hair, J. G., R. E. Anderson, R. L. Tatham & W. C. Black (1998). Multivariate Data Analysis. Upper Saddle River, New Jersey: Prentice Hall.

Hartson, H. R. (1998). Human-Computer Interaction: Interdisciplinary Roots and Trends. The Journal of Systems and Software, 43, 103-118.

Hartson, H. R., T. S. Andre & R. C. Williges (2001). Criteria for Evaluating Usability Evaluation Methods. International Journal of Human-Computer Interaction, 13(4), 373-410.

Hearst, M., A. Elliott, J. English, R. Sinha, K. Swearingen & K.-P. Yee (2002). Finding the Flow in Web Site Search. Communications of the ACM, 45(9), 42-49.

Henderson, R., J. Podd, M. Smith & H. Varela-Alvarez (1995). An Examination of Four User-Based Software Evaluation Methods. Interacting with Computers, 7(4), 412-432.

Herzberg, F., F. Mausner & B. Snyderman (1967). The Motivation to Work. New York: Wiley.

Hewett, T. T., R. Baecker, S. Card, T. Carey, J. Gasen, M. Mantei, G. Perlman, G. Strong & W. Verplank (1996). ACM SIGCHI Curricula for Human-Computer Interaction. Report of the ACM Special Interest Group on Computer-Human Interaction (SIGCHI) Curriculum Development Group, http://www.acm.org/sigchi/cdg/.

Hilbert, D. M. & D. F. Redmiles (2000). Extracting Usability Information from User Interface Events. ACM Computing Surveys, 23(4), 384-421.

Hirschman, E. C. & M. B. Holbrook (1982). Hedonic Consumption: Emerging Concepts, Methods and Propositions. Journal of Marketing, 46(3), 92-101.

Hirsh, H., C. Basu & B. D. Davison (2000). Learning to Personalize. Association for Computing Machinery. Communications of the ACM, 43(8), 102-106.

Hoffman, D. L. & T. P. Novak (1996). Marketing in Hypermedia Computer-Mediated Environments: Conceptual Foundations. Journal of Marketing, 60, 50-68.

Hoffman, D. L., T. P. Novak & M. Peralta (1999). Building Consumer Trust Online. Association for Computing Machinery. Communications of the ACM, 42(4), 80-85.

Holbrook, M. B. & E. C. Hirschman (1982). The Experiential Aspects of Consumption: Consumer Fantasies, Feelings, and Fun. Journal of Consumer Research, 9(2), 132-140.

Homburg, C. & H. Baumgartner (1995). Beurteilung von Kausalmodellen: Bestandsaufnahme Und Anwendungsempfehlungen. Marketing - Zeitschrift für Forschung und Praxis, 17(3), 162-176.

Hsu, M.-H. & C.-M. Chiu (2003). Internet Self-Efficacy and Electronic Service Acceptance. Decision Support Systems, 38(3), 369-381.

Hu, L. & P. M. Bentler (1999). Cutoff Criteria for Fit Indexes in Covariance Structure Analysis: Conventional Criteria Versus New Alternatives. Structural Equation Modeling, 6, 1-55.

Huang, M.-H. (2000). Information Load: Its Relationship to Online Exploratory and Shopping Behavior. International Journal of Information Management, 20(5), 337-347.

Hwang, M. I. & R. G. Thorn (1999). The Effect of User Engagement on System Success: A Meta-Analytical Integration of Research Findings. Information & Management, 35, 229-236.

Igbaria, M. & J. Iivari (1995). The Effects of Self-Efficacy on Computer Usage. Omega, 23(6), 587-605.

Igbaria, M., J. Iivari & H. Maragahh (1995). Why Do Individuals Use Computer Technology? A Finnish Case Study. Information & Management, 29(5), 227-238.

ISO (1998). International Standards Organisation. 9241-11 Ergonomic Requirements for Office Work with Visual Display Terminals - Part 11 Guidance on Usability.

ISO/IEC (1991). ISO/IEC 9126. Software Product Evaluation - Quality Characteristics and Guidelines for Their Use.

Ivory, M. Y. (2003). Automated Web Site Evaluation. Researchers' and Practitioners' Perspectives. Dordrecht, London: Kluwer Academic Publishers.

Ivory, M. Y. & M. A. Hearst (2001). The State of the Art in Automating Usability Evaluation of User Interfaces. ACM Computing Surveys, 33(4), 470-516.

Ivory, M. Y., R. R. Sinha & M. A. Hearst (2000). Preliminary Findings on Quantitative Measures for Distinguishing Highly Rated Information-Centric Web Pages. In: Proceedings of 6th Conference on Human Factors and the Web, Austin, USA.

Ivory, M. Y., R. R. Sinha & M. A. Hearst (2001). Empirically Validated Web Page Design Metrics. In: ACM SIGCHI, Seattle, USA.

Jacobsen, N. E. & B. E. John (2000). Two Case Studies in Using Cognitive Walkthrough for Interface Evaluation. School of Computer Science Technical Report CMU-CS-00-132. Pittsburgh, PA, Carnegie Mellon University.

Jeong, M. & C. U. Lambert (2001). Adaptation of an Information Quality Framework to Measure Customers' Behavioral Intentions to Use Lodging Web Sites. International Journal of Hospitality Management, 20(2), 129-146.

Johnson, K. L. & M. M. Misic (1999). Benchmarking: A Tool for Web Site Evaluation and Improvement. Internet Research: Applications and Policy, 9(5), 383-392.

Jones, C. D., S. J. Hollenhorst, F. Perna & S. Selin (2000). Validation of the Flow Theory in an on-Site Whitewater Kayaking Setting. Journal of Leisure Research, 32(2), 247-261.

Jung, T. H. & R. Butler (2000). Perceptions of Marketing Managers of the Effectiveness of the Internet in Tourism and Hospitality. Information Technology & Tourism, 3(3/4), 167-176.

Jutla, D., P. Bodorik & Y. Wang (1999). Developing Internet E-Commerce Benchmarks. Information Systems, 24(6), 475-493.

Katerattanakul, P. (2002). Framework of Effective Web Site Design for Business-to-Consumer Internet Commerce. Information & Management, 40(1), 57-71.

Kauffman, R. J. & A. A. Techatassanasoontorn (2005). International Diffusion of Digital Mobile Technology: A Coupled-Hazard State-Based Approach. Information Technology and Management, 6(2-3), 253-292.

Kim, S. & L. Stoel (2004). Apparel Retailers: Website Quality Dimensions and Satisfaction. Journal of Retailing & Consumer Services, 11(2), 109-118.

Kimery, K. M. & M. McCord (2002). Third-Party Assurances: Mapping the Road to Trust in E-Retailing. Journal of Information Technology Theory and Application (JITTA), 4(2), 63-82.

King, A. B. (2003). Flow in Web Design. In A. B. King (ed.): Speed up Your Site: Web Site Optimization. Indianapolis: New Riders.

Kirakowski, J. (2003). Using ISO 13 407 as a Guide to Personal Knowledge and Competence. http://www.ucc.ie/hfrg/resources/iso13407_intro.html.

Kline, R. B. (1998). Principles and Practice of Structural Equation Modeling. New York: Guilford Press.

Konana, P. & S. Balasubramanian (2005). The Social-Economic-Psychological Model of Technology Adoption and Usage: An Application to Online Investing. Decision Support Systems, 39(3), 505-524.

Korzaan, M. L. (2003). Going with the Flow: Predicting Online Purchase Intentions. Journal of Computer Information Systems, 43(4), 25-31.

Kosala, R. & H. Blockeel (2000). Web Mining Research: A Survey. SIGKDD Explorations, 2(1), 1-15.

Koufaris, M. & W. Hampton-Sosa (2004). The Development of Initial Trust in an Online Company by New Customers. Information & Management, 41(3), 377-397.

Krippendorff, K. (2004). Content Analysis: An Introduction to its Methodology. Thousand Oaks: Sage Publications.

Kroeber-Riel, W. & P. Weinberg (1996). Konsumentenverhalten. Munich: Franz Vahlen.

Kucuk, S. U. & M. Arslan (2000). A Cross Cultural Comparison of Consumers' Acceptance of the Web Marketing Facilities. Journal of Euromarketing, 9(3), 27-43.

Kumar, N. (2005). Personalization Systems and Their Deployment as Web Site Interface Design Decisions. In Y. Gao (ed.): Web Systems Design and Online Consumer Behavior. Hershey, USA: Idea Group Publ.

Laros, F. J. M. & J.-B. E. M. Steenkamp (2005). Emotions in Consumer Behavior: A Hierarchical Approach. Journal of Business Research, 58(10), 1437-1445.

Lederer, A. L., D. J. Maupin, M. P. Sena & Y. Zhuang (2000). The Technology Acceptance Model and the World Wide Web. Decision Support Systems, 29(3), 269-282.

Lee, M. K. O., C. M. K. Cheung & Z. Chen (2005). Acceptance of Internet-Based Learning Medium: The Role of Extrinsic and Intrinsic Motivation. Information & Management, 42(8), 1095-1104.

Lee, Y. & K. A. Kozar (2005). Investigating the Effect of Website Quality on E-Business Success: An Analytic Hierarchy Process (AHP) Approach. Decision Support Systems, 42, 1383–1401.

Legris, P., J. Ingham & P. Collerette (2003). Why Do People Use Information Technology? A Critical Review of the Technology Acceptance Model. Information & Management, 40(3), 191-204.

Lekakos, G. & G. M. Giaglis (2006). Improving the Prediction Accuracy of Recommendation Algorithms: Approaches Anchored on Human Factors. Interacting with Computers, 18(3), 410-431.

Lewis, J. R. (1995). IBM Computer Usability Satisfaction Questionnaires: Psychometric Evaluation and Instructions for Use. International Journal of Human-Computer Interaction, 7(1), 57-78.

Liang, T.-P. & J.-S. Huang (1998). An Empirical Study on Consumer Acceptance of Products in Electronic Markets: A Transaction Cost Model. Decision Support Systems, 24, 29-43.

Lin, W. T. & B. B. Shao (2000). The Relationship between User Participation and System Success: A Simultaneous Contingency Approach. Information & Management, 37, 283-295.

Lin, X. H., Y.-Y. Choong & G. Salvendy (1997). A Proposed Index of Usability: A Method for Comparing the Relative Usability of Different Software Systems Questionnaires. Behaviour & Information Technology, 16(4/5), 267-278.

Lindgaard, G. (1994). Usability Testing and System Evaluation. A Guide for Designing Useful Computer Systems. London, Glasgow: Chapman & Hall.

List, D. (2005). Know Your Audience: A Practical Guide to Media Research. New Zealand: Original Books.

Liu, J., C. K. Wong & K. K. Hui (2003). An Adaptive User Interface Based on Personalized Learning. IEEE Intelligent Systems, 18(2), 52-57.

Loiacono, E. T., R. T. Watson & D. L. Goodhue (2000). Webqual: A Measure of Web Site Quality. Working Paper 2000-126-0., University of Georgia.

Lynch, J. G. & D. Ariely (2000). Wine Online: Search Costs Affect Competition on Price, Quality, and Distribution. Marketing Science, 19(1), 83-103.

Lynch, J. G. & T. K. Srull (1982). Memory and Attentional Factors in Consumer Choice: Concepts and Research Methods. Journal of Consumer Research, 9(1), 18-37.

Marcussen, C. H. (2006). Trends in European Internet Distribution - of Travel and Tourism Services. http://www.crt.dk/uk/staff/chm/trends.htm.

Marsh, H. W., J. R. Balla & R. P. McDonald (1988). Goodness-of-Fit Indexes in Confirmatory Factor Analysis: The Effect of Sample Size. Psychological Bulletin, 103(3), 391-410.

Marsh, T. & P. Wright (1999). Co-Operative Evaluation of a Desktop Virtual Reality System. In M. Harrison and S. Smith (eds.): Workshop on User Centered Design and Implementation of Virtual Environments, pp. 99-108. The University of York.

Mazanec, J. A. (1982). Practising the Causal Approach to Consumer Behavior Model Building: An Example from Tourism Research. Der Markt, 84(4), 127-133.

McAlister, L. & E. Pessemier (1982). Variety Seeking Behavior: An Interdisciplinary Review. Journal of Consumer Research (pre-1986), 9(3), 311-322.

McGill, T., V. Hobbs & J. Klobas (2003). User-Developed Applications and Informations Systems Success: A Test of DeLone and McLean's Model. Information Resources Management Journal, 16(1), 24-45.

McKinney, V., K. Yoon & F. Zahedi (2002). The Measurement of Web-Customer Satisfaction: An Expectation and Disconfirmation Approach. Information Systems Research, 13(3), 296-315.

Middleton, V. T. (1995). Marketing in Travel and Tourism. Oxford: Butterworth Heinemann.

Molesworth, M. & J.-P. Suortti (2001). Buying Cars Online: The Adoption of the Web for High-Involvement, High-Cost Purchases. Journal of Consumer Behaviour, 2(2), 155-168.

Moon, J.-W. & Y.-G. Kim (2001). Extending the TAM for a World-Wide-Web Context. Information & Management, 38(4), 217-230.

Morosan, C. & M. Jeong (2006). Understanding Travelers' Adoption of Hotel Reservation Web Sites. In M. Hitz, M. Sigala and J. Murphy (eds.): Information and Communication Technologies in Tourism, Lausanne, Switzerland.

Muylle, S., R. Moenaert & M. Despontin (2004). The Conceptualization and Empirical Validation of Web Site User Satisfaction. Information & Management, 41(5), 543-560.

Mycoted (2004). Creativity & Innovation in Science & Technology: Browsing. http://www.mycoted.com/creativity/techniques/browsing.php.

Myers, M. D. (2005). Qualitative Research in Information Systems. http://www.qual.auckland.ac.nz/.

Negash, S., T. Ryan & M. Igbaria (2003). Quality and Effectiveness in Web-Based Customer Support Systems. Information & Management, 40, 757-768.

Nestorov, S. & S. Tsur (1999). Integrating Data Mining with Relational DBMS: A Tightly-Coupled Approach. In R. Y. Pinter and S. Tsur (eds.): 4th Workshop on Next Generation Information Technologies and Systems (NGITS), 295-311.

Neumann, W. L. (1997). Social Research Methods: Qualitative and Quantitative Approaches. Boston: Allyn and Bacon.

Nielsen, J. (1993). Usability Engineering. Boston, MA: Academic Press, Harcourt Brace & Company.

Norman, D. A. (2004). Emotional Design. Why We Love (or Hate) Everyday Things. New York: Basic Books.

Norman, G. & D. Streiner (2003). Path Analysis and Structural Equation Modeling. In: PDQ Statistics. BC Decker.

Novak, T. P., D. L. Hoffman & A. Duchacek (2003). The Influence of Goal-Directed and Experiental Activities on Online Flow Experiences. Journal of Consumer Psychology, 13(1&2), 3-16.

Novak, T. P., D. L. Hoffman & Y.-F. Yung (2000). Measuring the Customer Experience in Online Environments: A Structural Modeling Approach. Marketing Science, 19(1), 22-42.

O'Keefe, R. M. & T. McEachern (1998). Web-Based Customer Decision Support Systems. Association for Computing Machinery. Communications of the ACM, 41(3), 71-78.

Oliver, R. L. (1999). Whence Consumer Loyalty? Journal of Marketing, 63, 33-44.

Olsina, L. (2003). Methods for Quality Assessment of Web Sites and Applications. Presentation Held at the University of Trento, 02/04/2003.

Olsina, L. & G. Rossi (2001). A Quantitative Method for Quality Evaluation of Web Applications. In: Argentinian Symposium on Software Engineering (ASSE '2001), Bs. As., Argentina.

Ong, C.-S., J.-Y. Lai & Y.-S. Wang (2004). Factors Affecting Engineers' Acceptance of Asynchronous E-Learning Systems in High-Tech Companies. Information & Management, 41(6), 795-804.

Oppermann, R. & H. Reiterer (1997). Software Evaluation Using the 9241 Evaluator. Behaviour & Information Technology, 16(4/5), 232-245.

Palanisamy, R. & Sushil (2001). User Involvement in Information Systems Planning Leads to Strategic Success: An Empirical Study. Journal of Services Research, 1(2), 125-158.

Parasuraman, A., V. A. Zeithaml & L. L. Berry (1988). SERVQUAL: A Multiple-Item Scale for Measuring Consumer Perceptions of Service Quality. Journal of Retailing, 64(1), 12-40.

Parasuraman, A., V. A. Zeithaml & A. Malhotra (2005). E-S-QUAL: A Multiple-Item Scale for Assessing Electronic Service Quality. Journal of Service Research, 7(3), 213-233.

Pavlou, P. A. (2001). Consumers Intentions to Adopt Electronic Commerce – Incorporating Trust and Risk in the Technology Acceptance Model. In: DIGIT Workshop, New Orleans, Louisiana.

Pavlou, P. A. & L. Chai (2002). What Drives Electronic Commerce across Cultures? A Cross-Cultural Empirical Investigation of the Theory of Planned Behavior. In: Best Paper Proceedings of the Academy of Management Conference, Denver, Colorado.

Pavlou, P. A. & M. Fygenson (2006). Understanding and Predicting Electronic Commerce Adoption: An Extension of the Theory of Planned Behavior. MIS Quarterly, 30(1), 115-143.

Pearl, J. (2001). Causality: Models, Reasoning, and Inference. Cambridge: Cambridge Univ. Press.

Pedersen, P. E. & R. Ling (2003). Modifying Adoption Research for Mobile Internet Service Adoption: Cross-Disciplinary Interactions. In: 36th Hawaii Conference on System Sciences (HICSS'03), Hawaii: IEEE.

Pemberton, D., R. Rodden & R. Procter (2000). Groupmark: A WWW Recommender System Combining Collaborative and Information Filtering. In: 6th ERCIM Workshop "User Interfaces for All", Florence, Italy.

Perkowitz, M. & O. Etzioni (2000). Adaptive Web Sites. Association for Computing Machinery. Communications of the ACM, 43(8), 152-158.

Perugini, S., M. A. Gonçalves & E. A. Fox (2004). Recommender Systems Research: A Connection-Centric Survey. Journal of Intelligent Information Systems, 23(2), 107 - 143.

Perugini, S. & N. Ramakrishnan (2002). Personalizing Interactions with Information Systems. In M. V. Zelkowitz (ed.): Advances in Computers, 323-382. New York: Academic Press.

Purvis, R. & V. Sambamurthy (1997). An Examination of Designer and User Perceptions of Jad and the Traditional Is Design Methodology. Information & Management, 32(3), 123-135.

Raju, P. S. (1980). Optimum Stimulation Level: Its Relationship to Personality, Demographics, and Exploratory Behavior. Journal of Consumer Research (pre-1986), 7(3), 272.

Richard, M.-O. (2005). Modeling the Impact of Internet Atmospherics on Surfer Behavior. Journal of Business Research, 58(12), 1632-1642.

Riegelsberger, J., M. A. Sasse & J. D. Mc Carthy (2005). Rich Media, Poor Judgement? A Study of Media Effects on Users' Trust in Expertise. In: 19th British HCI Group Annual Conference, Edinburgh, UK.

Rieman, J., M. Franzke & D. Redmiles (1995). Usability Evaluation with the Cognitive Walkthrough. In ACM (ed.): CHI 95 Conference Companion 1995 ACM, 387-388. Denver, CO.

Rodgers, W., S. Negash & K. Suk (2005). The Moderating Effect of on-Line Experience on the Antecedents and Consequences of on-Line Satisfaction. Psychology and Marketing, 22(4), 313 - 331.

Rogers, E. M. (1976). New Product Adoption and Diffusion. Journal of Consumer Research (pre-1986), 2(4), 290-301.

Rogers, E. M. (1995). Diffusion of Innovations. New York: The Free Press.

Rowley, J. (2002). 'Window' Shopping and Browsing Opportunities in Cyberspace. Journal of Consumer Behaviour, 1(4), 369-378.

Runte, M. (2000). Personalisierung Im Internet: Individualisierte Angebote mit Collaborative Filtering. Wiesbaden: Dt. Univ.-Verl.

Saade, R. & B. Bahli (2005). The Impact of Cognitive Absorption on Perceived Usefulness and Perceived Ease of Use in on-Line Learning: An Extension of the Technology Acceptance Model. Information & Management, 42(2), 317-327.

Scharl, A. (2000). Evolutionary Web Development. London: Springer.

Schermelleh-Engel, K., H. Moosbrugger & H. Müller (2003). Evaluating the Fit of Structural Equation Models: Test of Significance and Descriptive Goodness-of-Fit Measures. Methods of Psychological Research Online, 8(2), 23-74.

Shang, R.-A., Y.-C. Chen & L. Shen (2005). Extrinsic Versus Intrinsic Motivations for Consumers to Shop on-line. Information & Management, 42(3), 401-413.

Shankar, V., A. K. Smith & A. Rangaswamy (2003). Customer Satisfaction and Loyalty in Online and Offline Environments. International Journal of Research in Marketing, 20, 153-175.

Shih, H.-P. (2004). An Empirical Study on Predicting User Acceptance of E-Shopping on the Web. Information & Management, 41(3), 351-368.

Shih, H.-P. (2004). Extended Technology Acceptance Model of Internet Utilization Behavior. Information & Management, 41(6), 719-729.

Shneiderman, B. (1992). Designing the User Interface. Strategies for Effective Human-Computer Interaction. Massachusetts: Addison-Wesley.

Skadberg, Y. X. & J. R. Kimmel (2004). Visitors' Flow Experience While Browsing a Web Site: Its Measurement, Contributing Factors and Consequences. Computers in Human Behavior, 20(3), 403-422.

Skinner, D. O., C. Tagg & J. A. Holloway (2000). Managers and Research: The Pros and Cons of Qualitative Approaches. Management Learning, 31(2), 163-179.

Smart, K. L. & M. E. Whiting (2001). Designing Systems That Support Learning and Use: A Customer-Centered Approach. Information & Management, 39(3), 177-190.

Smith, D. N. & K. Sivakumar (2004). Flow and Internet Shopping Behavior: A Conceptual Model and Research Propositions. Journal of Business Research, 57(10), 1199-1208.

Spangenberg, E. R. & K. E. Voss (1997). Measuring the Hedonic and Utilitarian Dimensions of Attitude: A Generally Applicable Scale. Advances in Consumer Research, 24(1), 235-241.

Spiliopoulou, M. (2000). Web Usage Mining for Web Site Evaluation. Communication of the ACM (Association for Computing Machinery), 43(8), 127-134.

Srivastava, J., R. Cooley, M. Deshpande & P.-N. Tan (2000). Web Usage Mining: Discovery and Applications of Usage Patterns from Web Data. SIGKDD Explorations, 1(2), 12-23.

Steenkamp, J.-B., Baumgartner, H. & E. van der Wulp (1996). The Relationships among Arousal Potential, Arousal and Stimulus Evaluation, and the Moderating Role of Need for Stimulation. International Journal of Research in Marketing, 13(4), 319-329.

Steenkamp, J.-B. & S. M. Burgess (2002). Optimum Stimulation Level and Exploratory Consumer Behavior in an Emerging Consumer Market. International Journal of Research in Marketing, 19(2), 131-150.

Stephanidis, C. (2001). User Interfaces for All: New Perspectives into Human-Computer Interaction. In C. Stephanidis (ed.): User Interfaces for All. Concepts, Methods, and Tools. pp. 3-17. Mahwah London: Lawrence Erlbaum Associates.

Steuer, J. (1992). Defining Virtual Reality: Dimensions Determining Telepresence. Journal of Communication, 42(4), 73-94.

Stewart, J. (2003). Investigating ICTs in Everyday Life: Insights from Research on the Adoption and Consumption of New ICTs in the Domestic Environment. Cognition Technology and Work, 5, 4-14.

Stewart, K. J. (2003). Trust Transfer on the World Wide Web. Organization Science, 14(1), 5-17.

Stockdale, R. & M. Borovicka (2006). Using Quality Dimensions in the Evaluation of Websites. In: Information Technologies in Tourism, Lausanne, Switzerland.

Stohr, E. A. & S. Viswanathan (1999). Recommendation Systems. Decision Support for the Information Economy. In K. E. Kendall (ed.): Emerging Information Technologies. Improving Decisions, Cooperation, and Infrastructure. pp. 21-44. Thousand Oaks, Calif.: Sage.

Stone, R. W. & J. W. Henry (2003). The Roles of Computer Self-Efficacy and Outcome Expectancy in Influencing the Computer End-User'S Organizational Commitment. Journal of End User Computing, 15(1), 38-53.

Suh, B. & I. Han (2002). Effect of Trust on Customer Acceptance of Internet Banking. Electronic Commerce Research and Applications, 1(3-4), 247-263.

Teo, T. S., V. K. Lim & R. Y. Lai (1999). Intrinsic and Extrinsic Motivation in Internet Usage. Omega, 27(1), 25-37.

Thompson, C. A., M. H. Göker & P. Langley (2004). A Personalized System for Conversational Recommendations. Journal of Artificial Intelligence Research, 21, 393-428.

Urban, G. L., F. Sultan & W. J. Qualls (2000). Placing Trust at the Center of Your Internet Strategy. Sloan Management Review, 42(1), 39-48.

van der Heijden, H. (2003). Factors Influencing the Usage of Websites: The Case of a Generic Portal in the Netherlands. Information & Management, 40, 541-549.

van der Heijden, H. (2004). User Acceptance of Hedonic Information Systems. MIS Quarterly, 28(4), 695-704.

van der Heijden, H. & L. Sorensen, S. (2003). Measuring Attitudes Towards Mobile Information Services: An Empirical Validation of the Hed/Ut Scale. In: 11th European Conference on Information Systems (ECIS), Naples, Italy.

van Waes, L. (2000). Thinking Aloud as a Method for Testing the Usability of Websites: The Influence of Task Variation on the Evaluation of Hypertext. IEEE Transactions on Professional Communication, 43(3), 279-291.

Vavra, T. G. (1997). Improving Your Measurement of Customer Satisfaction. Milwaukee, Wisconsin: ASQ Quality Press.

Veal, A. J. (1994). Research Methods for Leisure and Tourism: A Practical Guide. Harlow: Longman.

Venkatesh, V. & S. A. Brown (2001). A Longitudinal Investigation of Personal Computers in Homes: Adoption Determinants and Emerging Challenges. MIS Quarterly, 25(1), 71-103.

Venkatesh, V. & F. D. Davis (2000). A Theoretical Extension of the Technology Acceptance Model: Four Longitudinal Field Studies. Management Science, 46(2), 186-203.

Voss, K. E., E. R. Spangenberg & B. Grohmann (2003). Measuring the Hedonic and Utilitarian Dimensions of Consumer Attitude. Journal of Marketing Research (JMR), 40(3), 310-320.

Wallace, M., I. Maglongiannis, K. Karpouzis, G. Korzmentas & S. Kollias (2004). Intelligent One-Stop-Shop Travel Recommendations Using an Adpative Neural Network and Clustering of History. Information Technology & Tourism, 6(3), 181-193.

Wang, Y.-S. & T.-I. Tang (2003). Assessing Customer Perceptions of Website Service Quality in Digital Marketing Environments. Journal of End User Computing, 15(3), 14-31.

Wang, Y.-S., T.-I. Tang & J.-T. Tang, E. (2001). An Instrument for Measuring Customer Satisfaction toward Web Sites that Market Digital Products and Services. Journal of Electronic Commerce Research, 2(3), 89-102.

Weber, R. P. (1990). Basic Content Analysis. Newbury Park: Sage.

Wei, Y. Z., L. Moreau & N. R. Jennings (2003). Recommender Systems: A Market-Based Design. In: Autonomous Agents and Multiagent Systems (AAMAS), Melbourne, Australia.

Wierenga, B. & G. van Bruggen (2000). Factors that Determine the Success of a Marketing Management Support System. In B. Wierenga and G. H. van Bruggen (eds.): Marketing Management Support Systems: Principles, Tools, and Implementation. pp. 266-279. Boston: Kluwer Academic Publishers.

Wöber, K. W. & U. Gretzel (2000). Tourism Managers' Adoption of Marketing Decision Support Systems. Journal of Travel Research, 39(2), 172-181.

Wöber, K. W., A. Scharl, M. Natter & A. Taudes (2002). Success Factors of European Hotel Web Sites. In K. W. Wöber, A. J. Frew and M. Hitz (eds.): 9th International

Conference on Information and Communication Technologies in Tourism, pp. 397-406. Innsbruck, Austria: Springer.

Wright, S. (2002). Personalisation. How a Computer Can Know You Better Than Yourself. In: Multimedia Systems Conference, Southhampton, UK.

Wu, J.-H. & S.-C. Wang (2005). What Drives Mobile Commerce? An Empirical Evaluation of the Revised Technology Acceptance Model. Information & Management, 42(5), 719-729.

Yi, M. Y. & Y. Hwang (2003). Predicting the Use of Web-Based Information Systems: Self-Efficacy, Enjoyment, Learning Goal Orientation, and the Technology Acceptance Model. International Journal of Human-Computer Studies, 59, 431-449.

Yong, L. T. & T. E. Kong (1999). The Study of Cooperative Evaluation Approach on Internet Search. In: USM Computer Science Student Symposium on Computer Science and IT, University Science Malaysia.

Yoon, S.-J. (2002). The Antecedents and Consequences of Trust in Online-Purchase Decisions. Journal of Interactive Marketing, 16(2), 47-63.

Zaiane, O. R. (1998). From Resource Discovery to Knowledge Discovery on the Internet. Technical Report. Canada, Simon Fraser University.

Zeithaml, V. A., A. Parasuraman & A. Malhotra (2000). A Conceptual Framework for Understanding E-Service Quality: Implications for Future Research and Managerial Practice. Cambridge, MA, Marketing Science Institute: 1-46.

Zhang, P. & G. M. v. Dran (2000). Satisfiers and Dissatisfiers: A Two- Factor Model for Website Design and Evaluation. Journal of the American Society for Information Science, 51(14), 1253-1268.

Zinnbauer, M. & M. Eberl (2004). Die Überprüfung von Spezifikation und Güte von Strukturgleichungsmodellen: Verfahren und Anwendung. Schriften zur Empirischen Forschung und Quantitativen Unternehmensplanung, Ludwig-Maximilians-Universität München, Issue 21.

Zins, A. H. (2002). A Webscape Framework for Experience Goods and Its Implications for Various User Responses. In: Electronic proceedings of the eCTRL Workshop: User Modelling and Decision Making in Travel and Tourism Emergent Systems, pp. 49-53. Trento, Italy.

Zuckerman, M. (1979). Sensation Seeking: Beyond the Optimal Level of Arousal. Hillsdale, NJ: Lawrence Erlbaum.

Appendix

Interview Guide for the Expert Interviews

First, the purpose of the study and the user evaluation was outlined. Second, a definition of each of the constructs was given to ensure that interviewer and interviewee talk about the same topic.

(**Ease of Use:** the system's use is possible without great effort, the system's use is easy to learn, navigation path is clear

Usefulness: using a specific application will help to solve a specific task satisfactorily (accurate, meaningful, helpful information))

- Do you think Ease of Use and Usefulness serve as preconditions to achieve web site satisfaction? (meaning the web site has to be at least easy to use and useful to avoid dissatisfaction.)

(**Trust:** in that sense that personal data is treated carefully, if it is an e-commerce site payment is processed securely)

- Do you think people realise or take attention to if they deal with an https site?
- Do you think that people avoid buying something via the Internet because of security concerns?

(**Exploratory browsing:** interaction process, search process, satisfy curiosity, always know about the latest trends, offers, fun, joy of discovery, exciting, discover novelties)

- Do you think that factor has an impact on web site satisfaction (either in a positive or negative way)?

- Finally, are there are any additional factors you would consider as crucial for web site satisfaction?

Learn@WU Questionnaire

Herzlich Willkommen zur Befragung über Learn@WU

Das Institut für Tourismus führt in Zusammenarbeit mit Learn@WU eine Studie über die Zufriedenheit mit Web-Angeboten durch. Ihre Daten werden vollkommen anonym ausgewertet. Als Dankeschön für die Teilnahme an der Befragung werden unter allen Teilnehmern 30 x 2 Kinogutscheine verlost!

Zuallerst bitten wir Sie, dass Sie sich in folgende Situation versetzen:

Stellen Sie sich vor, Sie wollen in Kürze zur Prüfung "Marketing I" an der WU antreten. Daher möchten Sie sich mit Hilfe von Learn@WU einen Überblick über den Prüfungsstoff verschaffen.

Nun bitten wir Sie https://learn.wu-wien.ac.at/ zu öffnen (ohne das Fenster mit der Befragung zu schließen!) und sich einzuloggen. Versuchen Sie nun, sich von Learn@WU alle relevanten und interessanten Informationen zur Prüfung zu besorgen. Danach kehren Sie bitte zum kurzen Fragebogen zurück und beantworten Sie ihn (Beantwortungsdauer ca. 5 Minuten).

Vielen Dank für Ihre Teilnahme!

Nachdem Sie nun die Unterlagen mithilfe von Learn@WU gesucht haben, beantworten Sie bitte die nachfolgenden Fragen.

Je nach Zutreffen der einzelnen Aussagen auf das Web-Angebot Learn@WU stufen Sie bitte die Antworten auf der vorgegebenen Skala ab.

	stimme sehr zu	stimme eher zu	stimme eher nicht zu	stimme gar nicht zu
Im Großen und Ganzen finde ich, dass dieses Web-Angebot leicht zu bedienen ist.	O	O	O	O
Dieses Web-Angebot ist benutzerfreundlich.	O	O	O	O

	stimme sehr zu	stimme eher zu	stimme eher nicht zu	stimme gar nicht zu
Die Struktur dieses Web-Angebots ist verwirrend.	O	O	O	O
Die Bedienung von Learn@WU ist von neuen Benutzern leicht zu erlernen.	O	O	O	O

Je nach Zutreffen der einzelnen Aussagen auf das Web-Angebot Learn@WU stufen Sie bitte die Antworten auf der vorgegebenen Skala ab.

	stimme sehr zu	stimme eher zu	stimme eher nicht zu	stimme gar nicht zu
Im Großen und Ganzen empfinde ich dieses Web-Angebot als nützlich.	O	O	O	O
Die Benutzung von Learn@WU hat mir die Suche nach Lernunterlagen wesentlich erleichtert.	O	O	O	O
Dieses Web-Angebot ermöglicht es mir, rasch die für mich interessanten Informationen zu finden.	O	O	O	O
Dieses Web-Angebot erhöht die Qualität meiner Informationssuche.	O	O	O	O

Je nach Zutreffen der einzelnen Aussagen auf das Web-Angebot Learn@WU stufen Sie bitte die Antworten auf der vorgegebenen Skala ab.

	stimme sehr zu	stimme eher zu	stimme eher nicht zu	stimme gar nicht zu
Dieses Web-Angebot bringt mich auf neue Ideen.	O	O	O	O
Dieses Web-Angebot fördert meine Kreativität.	O	O	O	O
Dieses Web-Angebot macht erfinderisch.	O	O	O	O

Je nach Zutreffen der einzelnen Aussagen auf das Web-Angebot Learn@WU stufen Sie bitte die Antworten auf der vorgegebenen Skala ab.

	stimme sehr zu	stimme eher zu	stimme eher nicht zu	stimme gar nicht zu
Dieses Web-Angebot vermittelt das Gefühl, dass mit meinen persönlichen Daten mit größter Sorgfalt umgegangen wird.	O	O	O	O
Ich vertraue den auf Learn@WU angegebenen Informationen.	O	O	O	O
Ich habe das Gefühl, dass dieses Web-Angebot sicher ist.	O	O	O	O
Dieses Web-Angebot vermittelt das Gefühl, dass es mit den besten Sicherheitsstandards ausgestattet ist.	O	O	O	O
Die Vorschläge (Suchergebnisse) des Web-Angebots waren für mich nachvollziehbar.	O	O	O	O

Je nach Zutreffen der einzelnen Aussagen auf das Web-Angebot Learn@WU stufen Sie bitte die Antworten auf der vorgegebenen Skala ab.

	stimme sehr zu	stimme eher zu	stimme eher nicht zu	stimme gar nicht zu
Der Besuch dieses Web-Angebots war eine willkommene Abwechslung für mich.	O	O	O	O
Dieses Web-Angebot hat mich inspiriert.	O	O	O	O
Dieses Web-Angebot hat meine Neugier geweckt.	O	O	O	O
Die Benutzung von Learn@WU war spannend für mich.	O	O	O	O
Dieses Web-Angebot hat mir einiges an Neuem geboten.	O	O	O	O
Die Benutzung dieses Web-Angebots war wirklich ein Vergnügen.	O	O	O	O

Je nach Zutreffen der einzelnen Aussagen auf das Web-Angebot Learn@WU stufen Sie bitte die Antworten auf der vorgegebenen Skala ab.

	stimme sehr zu	stimme eher zu	stimme eher nicht zu	stimme gar nicht zu
Ich bin mit dem Erfolg meiner Informationssuche zufrieden.	O	O	O	O
Im Großen und Ganzen habe ich positive Erfahrungen mit der Benutzung von Learn@WU gemacht.	O	O	O	O
Dieses Web-Angebot war in der Lage, mich von der Qualität der	O	O	O	O

	stimme sehr zu	stimme eher zu	stimme eher nicht zu	stimme gar nicht zu
Vorschläge (Suchergebnisse) zu überzeugen.				
Dieses Web-Angebot entspricht meinen Erwartungen.	O	O	O	O

Je nach Zutreffen der einzelnen Aussagen auf das Web-Angebot Learn@WU stufen Sie bitte die Antworten auf der vorgegebenen Skala ab.

	Ich bin sehr zufrieden	Ich bin eher zufrieden	Ich bin eher unzufrieden	Ich bin sehr unzufrieden
Wie ist Ihr Gesamteindruck in Bezug auf das Web-Angebot?	O	O	O	O

Je nach Zutreffen der einzelnen Aussagen auf das Web-Angebot Learn@WU stufen Sie bitte die Antworten auf der vorgegebenen Skala ab.

	stimme sehr zu	stimme eher zu	stimme eher nicht zu	stimme gar nicht zu
Dieses Web-Angebot kann ich nur weiterempfehlen.	O	O	O	O
Ich werde dieses Web-Angebot wieder aufrufen.	O	O	O	O
In Zukunft werde ich dieses Web-Angebot noch öfters benutzen.	O	O	O	O

Je nach Zutreffen der einzelnen Aussagen auf das Web-Angebot Learn@WU stufen Sie bitte die Antworten auf der vorgegebenen Skala ab.

	stimme sehr zu	stimme eher zu	stimme eher nicht zu	stimme gar nicht zu
Ich bin aufgrund vergangener Nutzung mit Learn@WU vertraut.	O	O	O	O

Je nach Zutreffen der einzelnen Aussagen auf Ihr Verhalten in Bezug auf das WWW, stufen Sie bitte Ihre Antworten auf der vorgegebenen Skala ab.

	Täglich	Mehrmals pro Woche	Mehrmals pro Monat	Seltener
Wie oft benutzen Sie das WWW im Durchschnitt?	O	O	O	O
	Sehr erfahren	Erfahren	Wenig erfahren	Nicht erfahren
Würden Sie sich selbst als erfahrene/n WWW Nutzer/in bezeichnen?	O	O	O	O

Je nach Zutreffen der einzelnen Aussagen auf Ihr Verhalten in Bezug auf das WWW, stufen Sie bitte Ihre Antworten auf der vorgegebenen Skala ab.

	stimme sehr zu	stimme eher zu	stimme eher nicht zu	stimme gar nicht zu
Das WWW für diese Art von Aufgabe zu verwenden, halte ich für nützlich.	O	O	O	O
Die Informationssuche im WWW ist für mich mit einem zu hohen Zeitaufwand verbunden.	O	O	O	O
Ich finde es nützlich, mir	O	O	O	O

	stimme sehr zu	stimme eher zu	stimme eher nicht zu	stimme gar nicht zu
Lernunterlagen im WWW zu besorgen.				

Beantworten Sie nun bitte zum Abschluß noch einige Fragen zu Ihrer Person.

Ich bin:

- weiblich
- männlich

Mein Alter ist:

Meine derzeitige Beschäftigung ist: bitte ausw ählen

Meine höchste abgeschlossene Ausbildung ist: bitte ausw ählen

Falls Sie an der Verlosung von 30 x 2 Kinokarten teilnehmen wollen, geben Sie bitte Ihren Namen und E-mail Adresse an (Ihre Daten werden ausschließlich für diese einmalige Verlosung verwendet!):

Name:

E-mail Adresse:

Vielen Dank für Ihre Teilnahme!

Die Befragung ist nun beendet - Sie können das Fenster jetzt schließen.

Forschungsergebnisse der Wirtschaftsuniversität Wien

Herausgeber: Wirtschaftsuniversität Wien –
vertreten durch a.o. Univ. Prof. Dr. Barbara Sporn

Band 1 Stefan Felder: Frequenzallokation in der Telekommunikation. Ökonomische Analyse der Vergabe von Frequenzen unter besonderer Berücksichtigung der UMTS-Auktionen. 2004.

Band 2 Thomas Haller: Marketing im liberalisierten Strommarkt. Kommunikation und Produktplanung im Privatkundenmarkt. 2005.

Band 3 Alexander Stremitzer: Agency Theory: Methodology, Analysis. A Structured Approach to Writing Contracts. 2005.

Band 4 Günther Sedlacek: Analyse der Studiendauer und des Studienabbruch-Risikos. Unter Verwendung der statistischen Methoden der Ereignisanalyse. 2004.

Band 5 Monika Knassmüller: Unternehmensleitbilder im Vergleich. Sinn- und Bedeutungsrahmen deutschsprachiger Unternehmensleitbilder – Versuch einer empirischen (Re-)Konstruktion. 2005.

Band 6 Matthias Fink: Erfolgsfaktor Selbstverpflichtung bei vertrauensbasierten Kooperationen. Mit einem empirischen Befund. 2005.

Band 7 Michael Gerhard Kraft: Ökonomie zwischen Wissenschaft und Ethik. Eine dogmenhistorische Untersuchung von Léon M.E. Walras bis Milton Friedman. 2005.

Band 8 Ingrid Zechmeister: Mental Health Care Financing in the Process of Change. Challenges and Approaches for Austria. 2005.

Band 9 Sarah Meisenberger: Strukturierte Organisationen und Wissen. 2005.

Band 10 Anne-Katrin Neyer: Multinational teams in the European Commission and the European Parliament. 2005.

Band 11 Birgit Trukeschitz: Im Dienst Sozialer Dienste. Ökonomische Analyse der Beschäftigung in sozialen Dienstleistungseinrichtungen des Nonprofit Sektors. 2006

Band 12 Marcus Kölling: Interkulturelles Wissensmanagement. Deutschland Ost und West. 2006.

Band 13 Ulrich Berger: The Economics of Two-way Interconnection. 2006.

Band 14 Susanne Guth: Interoperability of DRM Systems. Exchanging and Processing XML-based Rights Expressions. 2006.

Band 15 Bernhard Klement: Ökonomische Kriterien und Anreizmechanismen für eine effiziente Förderung von industrieller Forschung und Innovation. Mit einer empirischen Quantifizierung der Hebeleffekte von F&E-Förderinstrumenten in Österreich. 2006.

Band 16 Markus Imgrund: Wege aus der Insolvenz. Eine Analyse der Fortführung und Sanierung insolventer Klein- und Mittelbetriebe unter besonderer Berücksichtigung des Konfigurationsansatzes. 2007.

Band 17 Nicolas Knotzer: Product Recommendations in E-Commerce Retailing Applications. 2008.

Band 18 Astrid Dickinger: Perceived Quality of Mobile Services. A Segment-Specific Analysis. 2007.

Band 19 Nadine Wiedermann-Ondrej: Hybride Finanzierungsinstrumente in der nationalen und internationalen Besteuerung der USA. 2008.

Band 20 Helmut Sorger: Entscheidungsorientiertes Risikomanagement in der Industrieunternehmung. 2008.

Band 21 Martin Rietsch: Messung und Analyse des ökonomischen Wechselkursrisikos aus Unternehmenssicht: Ein stochastischer Simulationsansatz. 2008.

Band 22 Hans Christian Mantler: Makroökonomische Effizienz des Finanzsektors. Herleitung eines theoretischen Modells und Schätzung der Wachstumsimplikationen für die Marktwirtschaften und Transformationsökonomien Europas. 2008.

Band 23 Youri Tacoun: La théorie de la valeur de Christian von Ehrenfels. 2008.

Band 24 Monika Koller: Longitudinale Betrachtung der Kognitiven Dissonanz. Eine Tagebuchstudie zur Reiseentscheidung. 2008.

Band 25 Marcus Scheiblecker: The Austrian Business Cycle in the European Context. 2008.

Band 26 Aida Numic: Multinational Teams in European and American Companies. 2008.

Band 27 Ulrike Bauernfeind: User Satisfaction with Personalised Internet Applications. 2008.

www.peterlang.de

FSC
www.fsc.org
MIX
Papier | Fördert
gute Waldnutzung
FSC® C083411

Kolibri 360 GmbH
Ferdinand-Jühlke-Straße 7
99095 Erfurt, Deutschland
produktsicherheit@kolibri360.de

Druck:
CPI Druckdienstleistungen GmbH
im Auftrag der
Kolibri 360 GmbH
Ferdinand-Jühlke-Str. 7
99095 Erfurt